Small Business Tax Planning

Hh Harriman House

Harriman House is one of the UK's leading independent publishers of financial and business books. Our catalogue covers personal finance, stock market investing and trading, current affairs, business and economics. For more details go to: www.harriman-house.com

Small Business Tax Planning

All you need to know from start-up to retirement

By Russell Cockburn

HARRIMAN HOUSE LTD
3A Penns Road
Petersfield
Hampshire
GU32 2EW
GREAT BRITAIN

Tel: +44 (0)1730 233870
Fax: +44 (0)1730 233880
Email: enquiries@harriman-house.com
Website: www.harriman-house.com

First published in Great Britain in 2011
Copyright © Harriman House 2011

The right of Russell Cockburn to be identified as Author has been asserted in accordance with the Copyright, Design and Patents Act 1988.

ISBN: 978-1906659-39-4

British Library Cataloguing in Publication Data
A CIP catalogue record for this book can be obtained from the British Library.

Printed and bound in Great Britain by CPI Antony Rowe, Chippenham.

Contents

About the Author

Russell Cockburn B.Sc (Hons) is a former HM Inspector of Taxes providing tax consultancy and advisory services to other professionals, businesses, executives and private clients. He also provides a broad range of tax training, lecturing, writing and publishing services. Russell was also the author of the *ICSA Tax Guide 2003-4*, published for tax advisers and practising professionals.

List of Abbreviations

AIA = Annual investment allowances

BPR = Business Property Relief

CGT = capital gains tax

CT = corporation tax

CTAP = corporation tax accounting period

EBT = employee benefit trust

ECA = Enhanced Capital Allowances

EIS = Enterprise Investment Scheme

ER = entrepreneurs' relief

FYA = first year allowance

GAAP = generally accepted accounting principles

HMRC = Her Majesty's Revenue & Customs

IFRS = international financial reporting standards

IHT = inheritance tax

LLP = limited liability partnership

NIC = national insurance contribution

NMW = national minimum wage

PAYE = pay as you earn

PLC = public limited company

R&D = research and development

SDLT = stamp duty land tax

VAT = value added tax

VCT = venture capital trust

Preface

What this book covers

This book examines the tax liabilities and payments, and implications of these, that the owners of small businesses need to bear in mind from the time they start a business to the time the business is sold, wound up, or passed on. A small business is defined as one with a turnover below £5m and with up to around 50 employees.

This book takes you through the full life cycle of a business: from the day it is first set up, through the early stages when the business is growing, on into the (hopefully) profitable years and then to the latter stages when the owner might be looking to realise the business' value by making capital disposals either of assets or of the whole firm. After that I look at the implications of retirement and possible liabilities arising from selling or gifting the business to family members or others.

We will consider tax liabilities on the business owner, taxes arising from the running of the business, taxes on profits that the business may make and taxes on profits the proprietor takes for themselves. The book also reviews the various taxes that may arise when a business is sold, and what reliefs and exemptions might be available to offset those liabilities. I also give advice and guidance on dealing with the tax authorities on a day-to-day basis, and where problems or cash flow difficulties can sometimes arise.

There is a bewildering amount of information concerning tax available to the small business owner, much of which is spread over many different locations either on the internet, in booklets provided by Her Majesty's Revenue & Customs (HMRC), or in magazines and annual publications. This book brings much of it together in a simple summary to get you started in understanding your tax affairs and to provide guidance on what to do and when.

You can use this book as a quick source of reference about your business and personal tax affairs or as a guide to help you plan for your tax liabilities when your business is up and running. You will also find it of use as the business grows and then later on when you look to sell it or pass it on.

This book focuses on small firms but some of the material will be of relevance to larger businesses, especially when we deal with the investment reliefs that are available and the potential tax liabilities arising on the disposal of a business towards the end of its life cycle.

Use of the terms business and company

Though **business** and **company** are often used interchangeably, for the purposes of this book **company** is used to refer to a limited entity with an issued share capital, where personal assets are distinct from those of the business manager or owner (for more information see 'Limited Company' on p. 26). I use the term **business** to refer in general to all types of commercial firm.

Who this book is for

The book is for those looking for practical help and guidance about their business tax affairs. It is written for the small business owner/manager who runs their own business and deals with the day-to-day interaction of the business with the UK's tax authorities.

All businesses tend to go through fairly recognisable stages of development and many encounter similar problems, especially where tax is concerned. Planning for business tax liabilities – whether these are the taxes on profits, the taxes to be paid for employing staff or taxes on turnover – represents a major charge on any business and on managerial time. Planning how much the liabilities will be, when they will arise and what may be done to mitigate the impact of tax on the business is just good management. Tax should be regarded as just another cost of the business; careful attention to it from the outset will pay considerable dividends in terms of lack of problems later on.

How the book is structured

The chapters in this book follow the most common pattern of business start-ups and the growth of businesses over time. Most businesses begin with one person's idea for a product or a service and a wish to sell it. Frequently the business then grows into a partnership, or it turns into a limited company. However, some businesses will commence trading as limited companies from the outset.

I deal with tax affairs of the smallest businesses – normally sole traders – first, followed by partnerships and then on to limited companies. This represents the most common form of progression. Each chapter summarises the tax consequences of particular business structures, how to plan for them effectively, and also discusses tax planning and mitigation techniques which may be available to the business person from year-to-year. Of course many businesses will stay in one structure throughout their entire lives and in this case only specific chapters will be relevant.

The first part of the book looks at the differing tax consequences of the available business structures, and considers the tax incentives and investment reliefs that are available on business start-ups, and also examining the tax consequences and the compliance implications of the various types of business structure through the stages of a business' growth.

Having looked at the start-up stage I next discuss the compliance aspects of a business' tax affairs, dealing with the tax authorities and possible techniques to adopt when faced with enquiries from the authorities on the business' accounts or tax returns.

Part Two looks at the tax consequences of the various ways in which proprietors can extract profits from their business, the available means of doing so and how to plan effectively to reduce the tax burden with each type of profit extraction method.

In Part Three, we move on to look at business sales and gifts to family members or employees, and capital taxation issues such as capital gains tax (CGT) on business disposals and inheritance tax (IHT) on business gifts during your life or on your death. Most entrepreneurs perhaps do not give much advance priority to these latter stages but they can be the most important tax bills of all, so planning for them well in advance will often reap the largest rewards.

Finally there are two detailed appendices which summarise the rates of tax and allowances applicable to corporate and non-corporate small businesses operating in the UK today.

Introduction – Tax And Your Business

Taxation is an expense that all profitable businesses have to deal with, and for this reason it is a cost which should be planned for and managed like any other. If tax is not planned for properly it can be a significant burden on any organisation, particularly a new and growing business. You should from the outset consider all the various taxes that your business has to pay as an important part of your business plan. Factor them in as business costs to be provided for like any other and put funds aside for them regularly so that they can be paid as and when they arise. Failure to do this is probably one of the most common mistakes made by many new businesses and one of the most common reasons why many new business owners get into trouble with the tax authorities at an early stage.

> " Taxation is an expense that all profitable businesses have to deal with and for this reason it is a cost which should be planned for and managed like any other. "

My aim in this book is to try and show the owners of small businesses that there are many straightforward and legitimate methods of planning, organising and controlling your tax liabilities and also of managing your interactions with the tax authorities. These are methods that will help you to reduce your overall business and personal tax burden. I will also identify aspects of a business that you can talk to advisers about so that together you can save yourself money.

All too often tax advisers are seen as a necessary evil; you need them to help you meet your statutory obligations but you'd rather not pay for them until the last possible moment. I hope that by the time you have finished this book you will agree with me that tax is something which, if planned for properly, can be as much an integral part of your business as getting the right suppliers for your materials or setting the right prices for your products or services.

PART ONE

Setting Up A Business

1. Business Structure – Choices and Tax Implications

On business structure

Many businesses do not give much consideration to their structure at the start-up stage. *This is a mistake*. The structure chosen at the outset will largely determine how and when the first, and all subsequent, tax bills arise, what tax planning techniques can be brought to bear and what opportunities there are for mitigating tax liabilities. The business structure can be changed later on but that can be a lot more expensive than getting it right from the outset.

Selecting the right business entity

Take some time to consider what business structure will be right for your venture before you begin. The choice might appear obvious but sometimes making the wrong decision at the start can have a significant negative affect on the success of the business for years to come. The alternative structures available differ considerably in their tax implications and

> **"** Take some time to consider what business structure will be right for your venture before you begin. **"**

so the choice you make will affect how much tax and National Insurance Contributions (NIC) you pay in the future and when you will pay them.

There are a range of choices available for a trading venture and in this chapter we will look at the following:

- Sole trader

- Partnership

- Small limited company

Before deciding upon one of these options, the questions you should ask yourself are:

- What trading entity should I use?

- What are the alternatives?

- What will be the different tax implications and when will tax be due?

- Do different structures offer differing planning options?

- Can I easily change structure once I have made the initial choice?

This chapter will provide you with the necessary information to help you choose.

Changing the business structure

Many businesses move from one type of business structure to another as they grow. They may take in a partner or outside investor or involve a family member as a tax-effective move.

The change from being a sole trader in self-employment to using a limited company structure is probably the most common seen in the small business world, but it might be better to adopt a small limited company structure from the outset. Getting this choice right requires some careful thought and a good look at the tax implications of the alternatives that are available.

Sole trader

Introduction and definition

For the individual with a business idea and the skills to put it into operation the most common choice is simply to set up as a self-employed individual; to become a *sole trader*.

A sole trader, or sole proprietorship, is one where the business and the owner are indistinguishable: the owner has unlimited liability for the business because they *are* the business. The business may be named after the owner or it may run under a specific trade name, thus Russ Cockburn might trade as "Russ Cockburn – Plumber" or he might use the trade name "Incredible Plumbers & Co". Whatever the name, the identity of the business is that of the proprietor, and the person running the business *is* that business. Legally the two are one and the same.

This form of business structure has the benefit of simplicity because it is relatively easy to set up and run. It is also likely to be the most appropriate choice for the smallest of enterprises. Indeed, some people start a business almost without realising it. The transition from enjoying a hobby to running a small business can often be a gradual and almost unnoticed change that occurs whilst the individual is employed by someone else in a permanent role.

Setting up as a sole trader requires minimal form filling and has relatively few compliance obligations in comparison to other business structures. For example, as regards initial interactions with the tax authorities, the simple form CWF1 is used to notify the start of the business for both income tax and NIC.

But is setting up as a sole trader the correct choice?

All too often business are started without giving some attention to the alternative business entities that are available.

There will be some types of business for which a sole tradership may not be the right choice. A business with a high level of commercial risk or potential product liability problems would probably be better advised to start using a limited company structure in order to give the proprietor more legal protection in the case of errors or faults arising in the course of running the business.

Some small businesses are effectively forced to run their activities through a limited company as their customers will not use subcontractors who are not incorporated; this is common, for example, in the professional contracting industry where many large end-users insist that their subcontractors operate via their own limited companies.

Businesses which expect to make significant profits from the outset will also need to consider at the start-up stage whether or not using a limited company will offer them business and personal tax mitigation opportunities. This is discussed later in this book.

Immediate tax and compliance implications

The early days of a sole trader's business must involve some basic compliance activities to ensure that the business gets off on the right footing with the tax authorities. Much of this can be done online.

The business has to notify HMRC that it has commenced trading and this must be done within three months of the end of the month in which the business starts up, otherwise there can be a fine (currently £100) for failure to notify for NIC purposes.

There is a second deadline of the 6 October after the end of the tax year in which the business starts up for income tax purposes as well. Failure to notify within this deadline can carry a tax-geared penalty, so telling the authorities that the business has commenced is very important.

A business that expects to exceed the VAT threshold (currently £70,000 turnover per annum) will also need to register with the tax authorities for VAT so as to avoid late-notification penalties. There are some other criteria to be reviewed and HMRC provides a VAT registration tool on its website to assist with this (**www.hmrc.gov.uk/vat**).

There may also be other tax registration obligations if the business is to employ staff or construction industry subcontractors, because regular returns for these individuals have to be submitted and tax deductions may have to be made from their earnings and accounted for to the tax authorities.

A business that uses a tax adviser, perhaps an accountant, will need to make information about the start-up date available to the adviser so that they can make prompt notification to the tax authorities to ensure any penalties are avoided.

Once registered, a business will then need to prepare annual accounts and submit an annual self-assessment tax return to HMRC. To facilitate this process the trader will need to start keeping proper records of all business transactions, income and expenses, and ensure that these records will be adequate for the purposes of preparing proper accounts after the end of the business' first financial year, or possibly sooner if the accounting date chosen is earlier than this.

The HMRC website has a specific section on starting up a business (**www.hmrc.gov.uk/startingup**).

Hidden implications

Deciding to start in business as a sole trader means that you have already made important choices – changing your business structure from sole tradership in the future may bring tax consequences.

If you convert your business to a partnership later on this may entail passing over a share in the business assets or goodwill to the new incoming partners. Whilst this is not normally a major issue, it will have to be considered carefully at that stage and specific tax advice will be needed as there can be capital taxation implications to overcome.

If you convert the business to a limited company as it grows, this will probably prove more expensive than would have been the case had the business been run as a limited company from the outset. Some businesses never grow that large or never need limited company status, but it should be recognised that converting a business from a sole tradership to a limited company vehicle can bring tax consequences which have to be managed at that stage. These are not normally insurmountable and in most cases the transfer can be accomplished without painful tax liabilities arising, but again specific tax advice will be needed to accomplish this transition smoothly.

Taking profits and paying tax from a sole tradership

Profits can be extracted easily

A sole tradership offers you ease of extraction of profits from the start. There are no specific laws about when the proprietor can take money out of the business (although of course running up an unauthorised overdraft will not go down well with the bank manager).

The ability of a sole trader to withdraw profits from the business at their own discretion differs from the shareholder in a limited company, as will be discussed later. This means that the sole trader is sometimes regarded as having significantly more flexibility and control over their own finances, with fewer tax complications.

When to pay tax

A sole trader is taxable on their profits, which have to be computed according to *normal commercial accountancy* principles. It is sensible to make early provision for tax liabilities.

If the business is going to be profitable straightaway then it will be vital to have a clear idea of when the first tax bills will be payable. Income tax falls due on 31 January and 31 July each year as payments on account. Payments on account are normally set at 50% of the previous year's income tax liability so there are no payments on account during the first year of a business' existence as there will be no such prior year. Thus, for example, a business commencing on 1 January 2010 will have its first tax bill falling due on 31 January 2011.

The final tax liability for any tax year is paid on 31 January after the end of the tax year. Thus the final payment for tax year 2010/2011 falls due on 31 January 2012, with two payments having been made on 31 January 2011 and 31 July 2011.

The sole trader will also be liable for two separate rates of National Insurance, known as class 2 and class 4 NICs. Class 2 is payable monthly by standing order to HMRC and class 4 is payable on the January and July payment dates based on the submission of the annual self-assessment tax return. (For the applicable tax rates and amounts see the appendices.)

As a business grows, its turnover may rise above the registration threshold for value added tax (VAT) and so it may also need to register to charge VAT on its goods and services and for the submission of VAT returns. This threshold applies whether or not the business is incorporated. The 2010/11 VAT registration threshold is turnover of £70,000 per annum and this means that the business must register for VAT if the supplies it has made in the past year, or in the next thirty days, exceed this figure at the end of any month unless turnover is not expected to exceed £68,000 in the next year (the de-registration threshold).

Tax advantages and disadvantages of sole tradership

Advantages

- Running your business on your own means you are in complete charge of the business. You make all the decisions and reap all the benefits.

- Tax liabilities arise twice yearly on 31 January and 31 July and you have complete control over paying them and planning for them yourself. Tax does not have to be paid monthly (as it does under PAYE for employees for example) although it is sensible to regularly set money aside towards your tax liabilities.

- You can extract money from a sole trader business at your own discretion without paying tax at that point in time and there is no PAYE obligation in respect of your own drawings from the business.

- Being self-employed is often seen as a more flexible business structure, especially where income tax relief for expenses is concerned. A common perception is that the self-employed pay less tax than employees on equivalent earnings. This is probably less true today than it has ever been as a result of statutory changes over the last 20 years. However, it is perhaps still true to say that the allowable expenses rules for the self-employed remain somewhat more relaxed than those available to employees, especially in the area of travel costs where the self-employed may be able to obtain relief for home-to-work travel which is normally not available to the employee on PAYE.

Disadvantages

The sole trader carries full liability for the tax bills on their business profits, as distinct from a limited company where the tax on profits initially falls on the company itself as a separate legal entity. So, whilst having control can mean flexibility over payment it also means that the tax authorities will seek redress from the individual where liabilities are unpaid or paid late.

> **"** The sole trader carries full liability for the tax bills on their business profits, as distinct from a limited company where the tax on profits initially falls on the company itself as a separate legal entity. **"**

Personal liability for business debts is not something to be taken lightly, whether these be tax or other bills. The sole trader exposes themselves to unlimited liability and this may put their personal wealth and assets at risk if they do not carry adequate insurance protection. For this reason alone many small business owners consider the use of a limited liability vehicle in an attempt to gain some personal protection from such potential risks.

Key sole trader tax issues

The most important things to remember about tax when setting up as a sole trader are:

- Profits are liable to income tax.

- Provision should be made for tax payments in January and July.

- Class 2 and 4 NIC is payable. Class 2 is payable by standing order monthly, class 4 with the half yearly tax payments.

- Income tax is due on 31 January after the tax year ends and also on 31 January and 31 July as payments on account for the next tax year.

- VAT registration may be necessary if turnover exceeds the statutory threshold.

- There can be penalties for leaving it too late to tell the tax authorities that you have started up in business. Use the HMRC website to access and complete the necessary tax, VAT and NIC notification forms so you don't miss these deadlines.

Partnership

Introduction and definition

Rather than go into business alone, it is possible to start a business where ownership responsibilities, debts and obligations are shared. This arrangement is called a *partnership*. If the venture requires the different skills or capabilities of a number of individuals then this type of structure may be ideal. A partnership is normally simple to form, requiring only a partnership agreement and a joint bank account to get started.

A partnership is defined in law as that arrangement which exists when individuals *carry on a business together with a view to profit.* Although most partnerships will operate under the cover of a formal partnership agreement this is not strictly necessary. Indeed it is important to recognise that ordinary partnerships are not even a separate legal entity for the purposes of English law (as they are in Scotland).

Nowadays partnerships can involve individuals as as well as companies. The partnership involving *corporate* partners is currently becoming a more popular tax planning vehicle as profitable partnership businesses seek to utilise this structure as a means of mitigating the highest rates of personal income tax in the UK, which increased to 50% in April 2010.

There are two main types of partnership structure available:

1. *Ordinary partnership* (formed under the provisions of the Partnership Act of 1890).

2. *Limited Liability Partnership* or LLP (formed under the Limited Liability Partnership Act 2000).

The LLP offers a hybrid structure with the benefit of limited liability and yet without what some advisers would consider the restrictive structure of a limited company.

Of course you should take careful legal advice before going into partnership with anyone. Trust will play an enormous part because individuals in an ordinary partnership carry joint and several liability for debts and other business liabilities they incur.

Immediate compliance and tax implications

The business which begins life as a partnership has the same potential tax notification obligations towards the tax authorities as the sole trader. Notification must be made of the date the business started up and registration for income tax, NIC, VAT and PAYE must all be considered straightaway to avoid penalties and compliance problems with HMRC from the outset. Notification for income tax will have to made on behalf of each partner as well as for the business itself.

Additionally, of course, the business that begins life as a partnership, or indeed which converts to a partnership from a sole tradership, must also notify the tax authorities of this business structure and complete commencement documents indicating the nature of the partnership and who the partners are. This will also bring additional form filling and compliance obligations for both income tax and VAT, and again these can be accessed from the HMRC website (**www.hmrc.gov.uk/startingup**).

Hidden implications

Operating as a partnership might cause tax problems if/when someone decides to leave the business. When a partner leaves they are treated as ceasing to carry on the business and this can have specific income tax consequences for them in the same way as happens when a sole trader ceases to trade. Most importantly the timing of a cessation is crucial because this will affect when the leaving individual's final income tax liabilities arise and so this should be considered well in advance.

As partners are not jointly and severally liable for their income tax bills in the UK, it is important for the leaving partner to understand that they will be solely responsible for paying the tax on their profits. This should be clearly established before they leave and their share of profits up to the date of their cessation will need to be agreed formally among all the partners so that they are aware of their tax liability arising thereon. The partnership agreement should thus make it absolutely clear how the partners' individual income tax liabilities are to be borne, whether by the firm or by the individuals themselves out of their drawings from the firm, so that there can be no dispute at a later date.

When individuals form a partnership they will often become joint owners of the business assets, property and goodwill. When there are subsequent changes in the makeup of the partnership this can bring capital taxation liabilities among the partners. For example, when a partner leaves the partnership and sells his or her share of the assets to the remaining partners, this in principle brings capital gains tax (CGT) liabilities. These can normally be overcome by referring to specific arrangements offered by various HMRC Statements of Practice, which are available to alleviate these potential liabilities (more on this later).

Choices made at the early stage of the formation of a partnership about the structure in which assets are owned can also have important tax implications later on in your business life. For example, if you choose to retain your business premises outside the balance sheet, perhaps because you do not want to share their ownership with the other business partners, this might impact on the rate of Business Property Relief (BPR) you would achieve for inheritance tax (IHT) purposes – it could reduce it to 50% instead of the normal 100%.

Whilst this is probably not a major consideration at the early stage of business development, it could become a major headache later on if you have to restructure the ownership of the business properties, as that can itself sometimes trigger undesirable tax liabilities.

Tax responsibility of partners

Partnership businesses are liable to income tax on their profits in the same way as a sole trader. The partners in have to prepare a partnership tax return as well as having individual returns prepared for each partner. When partners share their profits among themselves they are taxed accordingly. Thus if three partners share profits equally then the division of the tax liabilities will fall equally on them in respect of those profit shares. They will also normally be liable to Class 2 and 4 NICs in the same way as sole traders are.

> Partners in business in the UK have no joint and several liability for their income tax bills, which means that each partner is individually responsible for their own tax bills on their profit share.

Partners in business in the UK have no joint and several liability for their income tax bills, which means that each partner is individually responsible for their own tax bills on their profit share. One partner cannot normally be sued by HMRC if the other partner does not pay his or her tax bill. However, ensure that all partners' tax bills are paid on time and computed correctly because if one partner gets into trouble with the tax authorities it may affect their ability to participate in the business as a whole.

There must therefore be clear agreements and understandings in place among the partners about access to drawings from the business on a regular basis, and clear provision should be made in the partnership agreement for setting aside tax reserves to enable the partners' individual tax bills on their shares of profits to be paid on time.

The partnership business will have to produce financial accounts and tax returns for its venture in the same manner as the sole trader, but additionally there is a partnership tax return to prepare annually, showing the allocation of profits amongst the members. The ratio in which profits are shared amongst the partners in the financial accounts will determine the ratio in which the taxable shares are allocated on the partnership's return, and so attention will need to be paid to this aspect when ascertaining the overall tax liabilities which are going to arise on the annual profits of the partnership.

Why use a partnership structure?

Use of a partnership structure can sometimes reduce overall exposure to NIC and in some cases may be used as a means of avoiding PAYE obligations, although this can be regarded as extremely provocative and controversial by the tax authorities. Some well-known and very large retail organisations have operated successfully as a partnership, the John Lewis retail business for example, involving all their workforce for many years with consequent savings in NICs paid by the workers and the organisation itself.

Cases have also been observed where contracting organisations, particularly in agriculture, have used a large profit-sharing partnership agreement to operate via quasi-franchise arrangements with a large number of independent subcontractors. This is only likely to be feasible where the workforce is fairly static and each member can show that they also have other sources of income as well.

Partnership agreement

A business venture can often involve differences of opinion about how it should be run or how profits should be shared. This is why it is always advisable to have a formal partnership agreement that can be referred to at such times in order to provide a formal framework within which such dispute may be resolved. If there is no formal partnership agreement the Partnership Act of 1890 governs what has to be done where there is a dispute. This can often have unpleasant and unfortunate financial and commercial consequences so is to be avoided if at all possible.

A partnership agreement is not obligatory for tax purposes but it will save a lot of trouble if there is ever a dispute among the partners, especially over the tax provision for the individual liabilities of each partner.

Capital taxes and introducing new partners

As a business grows it is common to see new members introduced to a partnership. Taking on a partner may cause tax liabilities to arise so it must be considered carefully. In a situation where assets or shares in assets are to change hands, CGT liabilities may arise on the existing partners or on individuals disposing of shares in assets to the new partners. In some situations it may be necessary for specific assets to stay in the hands of an individual partner rather than being shared among all partners in order to avoid triggering these capital gains liabilities, but this can in itself have awkward capital tax implications.

For example, where a business asset is held individually by one particular partner it may not qualify in full for Business Property Relief from IHT (which is normally a 100% relief). Owning an asset personally may often be preferred by older partners but they will be the very individuals for whom IHT relief is likely to be regarded as an important tax planning issue in the medium term.

It will be helpful if the ownership of valuable business assets, especially business property, is established and regularised via the partnership agreement at the outset, both for commercial reasons and also to avoid unexpected CGT liabilities. There are a number of HMRC working practices which act to alleviate the worst impacts of these charges and specialist advice should be taken to ensure that the benefit of these practices is obtained wherever possible.

Where new partners buy into a business the existing partners may be regarded as making a disposal of their respective shares in the business and its assets. In some cases this *sale* of a partnership share can trigger CGT liabilities which will need to be carefully planned for before the final decision is made. Timing such transactions can be crucial and careful attention should be paid to this aspect as an incorrect decision can cause a tax liability to arise much earlier than is sometimes necessary. A disposal at the start of a tax year will probably defer a liability for another year, whereas a disposal just at the end of the tax year will mean the CGT is payable a year earlier.

For family partnerships the introduction of new members is relatively straightforward but the ownership of the business and its assets will need to be considered carefully. When valuable assets change hands between family members (known as *connected persons* for the purposes of UK taxation), CGT liabilities can arise. There are some specific reliefs available to defer these liabilities and these should be used to facilitate the introduction of the younger members of a family into the business structure. Family partnerships will be regarded

> **It will be helpful if the ownership of valuable business assets, especially business property, is established and regularised via the partnership agreement at the outset, both for commercial reasons and also to avoid unexpected CGT liabilities.**

differently from other partnerships in this respect as HMRC will not normally seek to impose *market value* rules among or between non-family partners.

For example, where there are changes in the profit-sharing ratios or the respective shares in business assets HMRC will not normally seek to interfere in the agreed transfer prices and consideration changing hands among the non-family partners; the presumption being that non-family members will generally be operating at *arms length* – i.e. it is presumed that non-family members will exchange assets at their market value. On the other hand, such transactions among family members will be looked at more closely by HMRC in order to ensure that there is no tax avoidance motive behind them.

The family partnership

The simple partnership is a very common business structure in the UK for family businesses. Its popularity owes much to the ability of partners to spread profits, and hence income tax liabilities, around its members thus hopefully optimising the use of available tax reliefs, allowances and thresholds. Using such allowances effectively will reduce the overall family tax bill.

In recent years HMRC has taken an increasingly aggressive interest in this sort of *income shifting* strategy and in 2007 they even suggested that they would bring forward anti-avoidance provisions to prevent family members, particularly husbands and wives, sharing taxable profits in this manner. However, to date these proposals have come to nothing, so profits can still be shared among family members with considerable flexibility and hence tax savings. Care should always be taken, however, to ensure that there is evidence available of the involvement of family members in the business (commercial underpinning in this way is an essential building-block of all good tax planning).

" The simple partnership is a very common business structure in the UK for family businesses. Its popularity owes much to the ability of partners to spread profits, and hence income tax liabilities, around its members. "

In the traditional family business there are often no structured arrangements for drawings or expenditures, and this spreading of the tax liabilities will rarely be reflected in the financial arrangements among family members. One of the most common sources of dispute in families between the generations is caused by the perception of the younger generations that such arrangements can contain an element of unfairness and inflexibility. It is always sensible to have clearly defined and formulated profit-sharing arrangements in place among members of a family, just as it is in partnerships where the members are not related.

The family partnership is also popular because of the relative ease of setting it up at the start and the flexibility it offers when individual partners join or leave – it is flexible enough to enable the introduction of members of the younger generation to a family business in a gradual manner. The initial introduction to partner status can be as a simple profit-sharing partner with no entitlement to assets, or for longer-term capital profits. This gradual transition to partnership status is often more acceptable to members of the older generation.

Passing assets on to the younger generation has traditionally been facilitated within the UK's capital tax system by the availability of some particularly flexible CGT reliefs. This has changed somewhat following the demise in 2008 of CGT Taper Relief, which had been very popular. Its replacement, known as entrepreneurs' relief, is much less flexible (see later) but it is still possible to pass shares in a family partnership on to the younger generation using a specific relief known as holdover relief (this offers deferral of CGT liabilities).

The family partnership structure can also be a means of minimising potential exposure to VAT on activities where the requirement to charge VAT could severely affect the profitability of the venture. This is because different partnerships comprised of different members will normally be taxable as separate entities, so if the turnover of each entity is below the VAT threshold then VAT will not normally have to be charged to customers.

There are fairly stringent anti-avoidance provisions here, which could have an impact, so careful advice would have to be taken before adopting what HMRC can sometimes regard as an adventurous strategy to VAT mitigation. This is particularly relevant where a small business diversifies into a number of different activities.

Where trading activities are very price sensitive and the competition at local level is fierce, charging VAT (otherwise known as output tax) can severely reduce the profitability of a business.

This is because prices cannot be increased to reflect VAT as this would damage the competitiveness of the business' pricing compared to prices charged by rival businesses.

Output tax

Output tax is the VAT charged on business supplies, i.e. goods and services provided to customers. A business selling taxable services has to charge VAT on top of the net invoice price, currently at 20%. Hence a bill of £100 will total £120 and the £20 of VAT is owed to HMRC on quarterly VAT returns.

Tax advantages and disadvantages of partnerships

Advantages

The main tax advantage of a partnership structure lies in the ability to share profits among members in a manner which can reduce income tax liabilities. Two individuals have two personal tax allowances and two basic rate income tax thresholds. This makes the partnership structure particularly attractive to family members who can thereby reduce their overall tax burden when they are involved in the running of the business.

Where the profits of a business are shared among several individuals this may also facilitate the making of extra pension provision for retirement. Whilst this is perhaps only a secondary consideration when starting your business, having pension income spread among two or more people in retirement can mean a more effective use of personal tax allowances in the later years of your life than would otherwise be possible if just one person has the pension income.

Other tax advantages which a partnership can bring include the ability to benefit from additional CGT reliefs on business disposals. The main relief here is CGT entrepreneurs' relief, introduced in 2008, which is limited to £5m of capital gains per individual over their lifetime. Initially this relief was set much lower but it was significantly increased over two Finance Acts in 2010 and now represents a very important capital tax relief indeed for the small business entrepreneur. If a business disposal is going to bring gains larger than this then there is a clear advantage in having the business and its valuable assets owned by a husband and wife rather than just the husband alone. Gains not covered by this relief carry a CGT liability at 28% instead of the rate of 10% achievable with this relief, so adding a partner could mean a very large reduction in the overall rate of CGT liability on a business disposal.

Having a business run by more than one individual can also mean that other capital gains reliefs such as *Rollover Relief* may be used more flexibly. For example, if the business owners were to trade down to smaller premises in hard times it may be possible to obtain Rollover Relief for one partner against the acquisition of the new assets. The manner in which this particular relief is structured may mean that the relief is unavailable if all the assets are owned by a single individual and the sale proceeds are allocated to one person.

Disadvantages

Sharing profits can bring additional NIC liabilities. Self-employed individuals currently pay class 4 NICs on their profit shares at 8% between profits of £5,715 and £43,875 and at 1% on profits above this level (2009/10). Allocating profits to someone else means they suffer an 8% NIC charge, whereas if the individual concerned was already earning above the £43,875 threshold there would only be a 1% liability. From April 2011 these rates are also likely to rise by 1% across the board at the lower levels.

Additionally, the self-employed individual also has to pay class 2 NICs, at £2.40 per week in 2009/10.

Where a business is run in partnership there are extra tax compliance obligations to fulfil. A partnership tax return has to be submitted annually in addition to the tax returns for each individual partner and failure to do so carries penalties for each partner. One of the partners also has to take on the role of *designated partner*, meaning they are the person responsible for communicating with the tax authorities on behalf of the business.

Key tax issues of a partnership

The key tax issues when considering a partnership structure are as follows:

- Funds should be set aside to provide for partners' individual tax liabilities on their profit shares.

- Profits might be able to be shared among family members tax effectively, though the likely reaction of HMRC to this strategy should be considered. Partners all have to be actively involved in the business.

- Tax liabilities may arise when assets or partnership shares change hands.

- How profits will be allocated and taxed among the partners.

- Tax arises on profit shares so there should be proper agreements in place on profit sharing and partnership profit allocations.

- Who will own the assets and what tax bills will this cause, now and in the future?

- Should the assets be owned inside or outside the business balance sheet?

Limited Company

Introduction and definition

A limited company is a specific legal entity in its own right. Companies are registered by application to Companies House in Cardiff. A company is formed by individuals subscribing for shares in the company. These are normally £1 Ordinary shares but there can be many different varieties of shares and you should take specific legal and financial advice about the correct type of share structure that will be appropriate for the particular circumstances of your business.

Three reasons for using a limited company structure
1. Low effective rates of corporation tax (CT).
2. No NICs payable on dividends.
3. No income tax on dividends up to the higher rate income tax threshold.

A company is a separate entity or *person* for UK tax purposes and it pays corporation tax (CT) not income tax on its corporate profits. This is distinct from the taxes that will become due on you personally on any profits that you extract from the company either as salary, bonuses, benefits in kind or as dividends from the company's taxed profits.

Most UK limited companies are private companies owned by their shareholders, of which there are normally a small number. Public Limited Companies (PLCs) are companies whose shares are quoted on the stock exchange and which are publicly traded as a commodity. Private company shares change hands less frequently than shares in PLCs.

A structure for larger businesses?

There is a perception that a limited company might be more suitable for larger business concerns and that perhaps as your business grows it may develop into a limited company. Certainly larger business do tend to be run as limited companies, although there are some very large partnerships around, notably in the world of professional services and retailing. The limited company need not be the exclusive province of the large business though – many small businesses now begin life as limited companies.

Clearer ownership

A limited company provides a clear method of allocating ownership by reference to issued share capital. Many people prefer this to the rather looser commercial ownership arrangements that partnerships appear to provide. Having a set number of shares issued to each *participator* in the company provides a very clear method of dividing up the ownership of the business.

Company taxation

Company profits are liable to CT in the UK, as opposed to income tax. The company is a separate legal entity, which means it has its own profits and tax regime, and this is perhaps the most difficult aspect of the structure for the businessperson to come to terms with. The company's financial accounts will be prepared, its profits computed and a tax liability will arise on those profits. This tax bill will have to be paid by the company. The company will normally have to pay its CT bill nine months after its financial year comes to an end (as long as it is defined as *small or medium* for corporation tax purposes. A small company for these CT purposes is one whose profits are below £1,500,000 annually).

> **The limited company need not be the exclusive province of the large business though – many small businesses now begin life as limited companies.**

The immediate compliance and tax implications

As for sole traders and partnerships the business that starts up as a limited company must make all the normal notifications to the tax authorities that it has started in business and that it will be liable for CT, PAYE on the earnings of its employees and directors, and possibly VAT on its business turnover. It will also have to deal with Companies House on an annual basis, ensuring that it files its annual accounts and Companies House returns – this is in addition to filing its financial accounts, CT returns, PAYE returns and VAT with the tax authorities.

Again, advice on how to start doing all of this can be found on the HMRC website (**www.hmrc.gov.uk/startingup**).

The proprietors of a small limited company – its shareholders – will probably be company directors as well, and one of these will be the company secretary. These roles have important legal responsibilities towards the company, the other shareholders, any investors in the company, and any financial or other lenders. These are important and potentially onerous responsibilities not to be undertaken lightly and should therefore be entered into with proper financial and legal advice at the outset. In particular the directors of a company have specific legal obligations set out in the Companies Acts for record keeping and the conduct of the company's business. These must be adhered to carefully to ensure that the company is trading legally at all times.

Hidden implications

If you start your business as a limited company one of the most important choices you make will be the ownership of the business' major assets – whether they are put into the company balance sheet or kept outside of the company in your own hands. Making the wrong choice here can mean extra undesirable tax consequences later on.

For example, if you choose to retain your business premises outside the company's balance sheet, perhaps because you do not want to share their ownership with the other shareholders, this might impact on the rate of *Business Property Relief* you would achieve for inheritance tax (IHT) against any gifts of your company shares. For example, it will reduce the rate of relief to 50% of the property value instead of the normal 100% if you are a controlling shareholder in the company (you have more than 50% of the voting shares). However, if you are not a controlling shareholder then the rate of IHT relief could be reduced to zero if the property is held by you outside the limited company balance sheet.

It is also important to recognise that there is an inherent conflict here between the desire to achieve full IHT relief and the potential for CGT liabilities to arise later on. If the business property is owned by the limited company then on the sale of that property by the company any capital gain accruing will suffer CT inside the company. The net of tax proceeds are then inside the company and will have to be extracted by the shareholders, probably resulting in a further tax charge either to income tax or possibly to more CGT.

If the property were held outside the company then only one such disposal tax charge would arise but this would be at the risk of low or possibly nil IHT Business Property Relief. There is a trade-off to be considered here and the decision is never an easy one to make. It will probably be determined by your long-term plans for the business property and whether a sale is in prospect over the medium term or whether you will pass it on down the generations as part of the growing business enterprise in the future. Take careful advice before you finalise this decision. In practice the decision is often made for you by your lender if borrowings are to be secured on the property assets.

Extracting funds from a company means tax is due

Wherever any funds are extracted from a limited company by its directors and shareholders there is normally a tax liability on those individuals and sometimes on the company too. It is this aspect of the structure that needs to be properly understood before contemplating the use of a limited company.

Whether money is paid out as remuneration, loans, dividends, benefits in kind, salary or bonuses, there is the potential for tax to be payable either under the PAYE regulations by the company or by the recipient.

An individual pays income tax on their salary, bonuses or dividends according to the income tax self-assessment rules, and the PAYE regulations. Thus, if salary is paid out then the income tax and NICs are due every month from the company under the PAYE procedures as for any other employee. If dividends are paid out then the income tax is due

> **The owner-manager of a small limited company has some significant degree of control over how and when their personal income tax and company liabilities will actually arise and when they are then payable to the tax authorities.**

on 31 January following the end of the tax year in which the dividend is received.

This means that the owner-manager of a small limited company has some significant degree of control over how and when their personal income tax and company liabilities will actually arise and when they are then payable to the tax authorities. With an unincorporated sole tradership or partnership structure the tax bills relate to the profits made, not the funds accessed by the proprietor, so there is arguably less control over the timing of when personal tax liabilities will actually arise on the business profits.

This is often one of the reasons why many small business owners are discouraged from using a company structure. Their perception is that the structure is too cumbersome and complex for their business to utilise effectively. Whilst there is no doubt that it can be more complex, there is no reason why most businesspeople cannot use a limited company with ease; providing a few simple rules are followed it is reasonably straightforward to operate.

Tax reasons for using a limited company

There are three main reasons why using a limited company is an attractive proposition for many small businesses:

1. Low effective rates of CT.

2. No NICs payable on dividends.

3. No income tax on dividends up to the higher rate income tax threshold.

With higher rate income tax at 40% (50% for some) and small company tax currently set at 21%, for some individuals the use of the corporate structure can be tax effective. This is in addition to the dividends tax regime, under which no income tax is payable on dividends below the higher rate income tax threshold (currently set at £37,400 of taxable income) and whereby no NIC is paid on company dividends.

In Part Two I will show the effective rates of tax paid on extracting profits from a limited company via different methods, but at this stage it is relevant to point out that running a business as a small company entity can save some businesspeople significant amounts of tax and NIC once their business starts to make decent levels of profits.

With low profits in the initial years after start-up, however, the benefit of small company structure is probably marginal given that the rate of small company tax is now 21% and the starting rate of income tax is 20%.

When will the tax liability arise?

The small limited company will normally have to pay its first CT bill by the day which falls nine months after the end of its first accounting year. Thus the choice of business entity will have a direct bearing on when tax falls due and how soon. The limited company that starts trading on 1 January 2010 need not pay any CT until 1 October 2011.

It is also important to realise that if you use a limited company there will be two tax-paying entities, you and the company. The company will pay tax on its computed business profits. Once that tax has been paid then anything left can be extracted by you as dividends. However, salaries, bonuses and benefits in kind that you pay or make available to yourself from the company will act to reduce those profits, so there are a number of choices to be made here, each of which can have tax implications.

Whether using the limited company structure for small businesses will be beneficial or not depends upon just how much of the profits the individual shareholders wish to extract from their company for their own use. As profits rise significantly the retention of profits inside a company where they have suffered only CT at 21% can be perceived as a very attractive tax advantage. Extracting profits, with personal income tax rates as high as 50%, is seen by some as clear motivation to use the corporate structure for tax planning purposes alone. Of course, extracting those funds from the company later on either as distributions or as capital receipts on a winding up will still trigger tax liabilities. However, these may in some circumstances be as low as 10% if entrepreneurs' relief is available.

Who will own the company?

The limited company can give the business owner the capability to set up different types of ownership for the business via the use of different types and classes of shares and different rights attached to those different shares. Other special types of share can even be used to offer outside investors specific types of income tax incentives and reliefs, and thus provide a means of attracting outside funds to get the business off the ground.

For example, you can have shares which give full ownership rights over the assets of the company or you can have other shares issued which simply provide for the possibility of receiving dividends in the future and no other rights.

Companies which meet certain qualifying conditions can also raise capital under the Enterprise Investment Scheme (EIS). This special tax regime allows subscribers to the shares to obtain income tax relief at 20% of the amount invested – provided the relevant conditions are met.

Flexibility over timing of payments

The limited company can offer flexibility on the timing of the personal income tax liabilities of the owner manager. Remuneration can be paid at specific dates and this triggers the PAYE income tax and NIC liabilities. Or, to put it another way, not paying it will defer the income tax and NIC liabilities. Of course not paying salaries or bonuses means that the company is not getting any tax relief on them and the owner is not accessing the profits he is making, so there is a trade-off being made in this situation.

Limited liability

The most frequently quoted reason for using a company structure is protection from creditors. Whilst this may be useful in risky commercial sectors, similar protection can often now be achieved via the use of a limited liability partnership (LLP), so a company is not always absolutely necessary. Frequently banks and finance houses may insist on the use of a company structure as a condition of their investment in a new business venture.

Tax advantages and disadvantages of a limited company

Advantages

A limited company offers clear legal separation between the business and the proprietor. This arrangement can offer some specific benefits to the proprietor. In particular, having the profits of a business inside a company will mean that taxation liabilities can be restricted to company tax only, unless the proprietor extracts profits.

Companies can therefore be used for small business ventures and tax may only be payable at the small companies rate, which is currently set at 21% (this will change to 20% from 1 April 2011) and which is very much lower than the top rate of income tax, currently 50%.

A company enables the proprietor to determine largely at their own discretion when their personal income tax liabilities will arise because the proprietor can decide when and how to extract their profits (net of CT) from the business, or whether to extract those profits in a tax deductible form such as salaries or bonuses.

Using a company structure can also enable the owners of a business to divide it up into a number of shares among family members. These shareholdings can be large or small. The ability to have different shareholdings and indeed different share types offers the small family business a mechanism by which it can reflect the different involvements of family members with differing shareholdings and access thereafter to the value of the company and its assets and/or profits.

Disadvantages

Using a limited company introduces an additional level of complexity and bureaucracy to running the business. Its status as a separate legal entity brings with it a lot more form-filling and extra official returns to be completed annually, all of which means additional costs.

Some people also find the public disclosure aspects of filling accounts at Companies House rather unattractive. In reality this need not be regarded as a significant burden as most small companies can file abbreviated accounts with Companies House.

Key limited company tax issues

- A small company normally pays its tax bill nine months after the end of its financial year.

- Salaries or bonuses can only be paid out to employees and directors subject to the PAYE regulations, under which income tax and NICs must normally be deducted and accounted for to HMRC.

- Dividends are taxable on receipt by the shareholders and can only be paid out if there are profits in the company, and then only the amount after the application of CT can legally be paid out to the shareholders.

- If the shareholders borrow funds from a company there is normally a 25% tax bill due to HMRC from the company nine months after its year end. This *loans tax* is only repayable nine months after the end of the company accounting period in which the loan is repaid to the company.

Weighing up the different structures

Whilst many small businesses will still start out as sole traders or partnerships, the limited company option should always be considered from the outset, even if is quickly discounted as too costly.

It is not possible to give a hard and fast equation showing what structure is likely to be preferable. An example of how to do the mathematical comparison can be found in Chapter 3, but it is often necessary to make a large number of assumptions to effect those calculations, and in doing so they may become meaningless.

As something of a generalisation, it is probably true to say that for a sole trader making profits in the region just above £50,000 per annum it is likely that the use of a limited company may offer significant income tax and NIC savings over the medium term. As profits rise above this level it is likely that a company will become even more attractive.

Of course if the sole trader can bring in a family member as a partner or an employee to share in the earnings of the business then the mathematics change dramatically, especially if both partners are equally involved. This might well mean that the profit threshold at which incorporating the business becomes a sensible option rises significantly.

The potential tax savings from incorporation will have to be weighed carefully against the higher compliance and regulatory costs that accrue from running a business via a limited company structure. Anyone contemplating the choice will need to obtain clear estimates from their professional advisers on what the additional costs are going to be. Tax estimates against the forecast profits in the business plan should also be obtained, on the alternative basis of corporate and non-corporate structure.

Some businesses have to adopt a limited company structure

Some businesses will have to be operated via a limited company structure. In some industries, for example professional contracting and consultancy business, many large customers and main contractors will not use freelance individuals unless they operate via their own limited company. This is mainly because these large organisations do not wish to have employees on their payroll so that they have greater flexibility in their use of labour on their own contracts which can vary greatly in length and frequency. It is almost certainly also done to avoid the necessity to operate PAYE and NIC on their freelance subcontractors' earnings.

> **"** For a sole trader making profits in the region just above £50,000 per annum it is likely that the use of a limited company may offer significant income tax and NIC savings over the medium term. **"**

Legislation may affect the decision

There are some very specific pieces of tax legislation that may have an impact on the calculation of the tax liabilities of individuals operating a business through a company structure, most notably the Intermediaries Tax Legislation (commonly known as the IR35 rules). These can impose a form of PAYE on the earnings of companies run by one person before the earnings are paid out to their owners as dividends. There are also anti-avoidance provisions known as the Managed Service Company rules which seek to prevent the use of *umbrella* or *composite* companies by individuals in this situation.

Other structures

Sole trader, partnership (ordinary or LLP) or limited company will be the most frequent choice for most business start ups. However, there are a number of other possible start-up entities, some of which are only suitable for specific types of business and others which will probably only be relevant as a business becomes much larger.

Limited partnership

This partnership provides specific limited protection for investors in the partnership such that their liability for losses is effectively limited to the extent of their investment in the business. Special tax rules act to restrict the offset of losses incurred by members of such partnerships against their general income, mainly as the result of these structures having been utilised for tax avoidance purposes in previous years.

Broadly, loss relief is limited to the amount of the investor's original capital invested in the partnership. Relief may also be refused if the partner is not actively engaged in the business, this normally being interpreted by HMRC as spending at least ten hours per week on work for the business.

Company partner

A rather more innovative structure which is being employed by some businesses nowadays is the use of a *corporate partner*. This involves forming a company and adding it as a partner in a partnership structure. The company can then participate in the running of the business and receive a share of the business profits. The company's share will be taxed under CT rules and at company tax rates. This is becoming an increasingly popular method of reducing partnership tax liabilities in some industry sectors, and if you can cope with the additional administrative costs, and importantly if you can find a commercial reason to underpin the use of the company partner, then this could well save your partnership a lot of income tax.

Mutual concern

There are many businesses in the UK operated as clubs and associations where members have joined together to run a venture for their own benefit, often on a not-for-profit basis. These are commonly known as *mutual* for tax purposes. This term indicates that they are not normally regarded as taxable on their profits as these only arise from transactions amongst the membership.

Of course some mutual concerns, such as members' golf clubs, may well also trade with the general public and the profits on any of these transactions may well come within the scope of the tax regime on an apportioned basis of their income and expenses. Such mutual concerns often run their businesses via a special type of company known as a Company Limited by Guarantee. Here the owners of the business do not hold share capital in the company and have no legal exposure to any losses it may incur. Similarly their entitlements to capital on any winding up are strictly defined by law.

The mutual structure will not normally be available to profit-motivated businesses. Nevertheless, it remains an important part of the economy since many such organisations are major employers in their local communities.

Joint venture

This structure is most commonly encountered in the corporate sphere, where a joint venture is known as a consortium, but it can be used for quasi-partnership ventures. Where it is desired that several individuals wish to run a business venture together but have no wish to formalise their business relations within a strict partnership structure, a more loose joint venture arrangement may be suitable. Under this arrangement the individuals choose to share overheads and expenses, and pool their resources, but retain entitlement to income pro-rata to their specific efforts into the business.

In such situations it is common to see the work done invoiced separately by each individual to their personal customers, whereas expenses will be paid either individually or from a common pool. Hunting and shooting syndicates have customarily been run in this format in the UK. Commonly HMRC will accept the use of a partnership tax return to facilitate the submission of the necessary information to them for self-assessment purposes, but this is not strictly necessary and in some circumstances can even confuse matters from the administrative viewpoint.

Groups and consortia

When a corporate business grows to a significant size the use of separate trading divisions often occurs to enable the identification and control of costs arising from different business activities. Subsequently a group of companies under common control with holding companies and subsidiaries under common ownership may be utilised to provide decentralised managerial structures and clear lines of responsibility for different trading activities. This is known as a *group* for UK CT purposes and comes into its own as a business grows. A detailed discussion of groups is outside the scope of this book but it is a very useful structure when a business gets large and in particular enables companies to share loss relief and other expenses in a tax-effective manner.

A consortium is a joint venture among companies that are not normally members of a group. Any losses arising to the consortium company can be shared among the consortium members in proportion to their relative investments in the consortium company. Again these structures tend to be the preserve of very large businesses and are beyond the scope of this book.

Tax implications of business location

Most businesses start in a particular place because that is where the owner or manager is going to be working and that's where the customers will be found. However, choice of location might in some cases have an impact on tax liabilities.

Considerations when locating within the UK

Historically some parts of the UK have qualified as Enterprise Zones for the purposes of special tax incentives on capital investment, so care should always be taken to check that such incentives are not being missed when a business commences.

Some locations may be less tax attractive than others. The city of Nottingham recently announced that it may become the first city to impose a tax on *workplace car parking* for employees and it looks as though other cities may follow suit. Clearly the imposition of location-based taxes is something that any business will in future have to take into account.

The level of business rates and the availability of discounts in locations known as *economically disadvantaged areas* is certainly an important factor to take into account. Some business tax reliefs such as the Business Premises Renovation Allowances, available where business brings previously derelict premises back into commercial use, can only be obtained where the business is located in a defined geographical area.

Locating overseas

Some people perceive that locating their venture overseas may offer tax planning advantages. At times of higher tax rates in the UK businesses have sought to relocate overseas to avoid these extra charges. With the advent of the 50% higher rate of income tax in the UK in 2010 it seems possible that we may see such thinking become more widespread.

Setting up a business overseas, especially in locations where there are incentives to do so, has arguably never been easier. However, operating a business abroad in a manner which is legitimately outside the scope of UK taxation is far from straightforward and will require careful planning.

Firstly, any self-employed person who simply registers their business overseas and continues to run it from a base in the UK (technically known as a permanent establishment), will almost certainly still be within the scope of UK taxation. Avoiding UK tax on the profits of a self-employed business run from a base here will be very difficult.

The self-employed person starting up overseas but having been previously a UK resident (for tax purposes) will need to establish clear non-resident status for UK tax purposes and also establish that they no longer have a permanent establishment or base of operations in the UK. Only in this manner will it be possible to convince the UK tax authorities that in fact there is no liability to tax in the UK. The practicalities of doing so, and the costs involved, often outweigh the perceived advantages of the new set-up strategy. This is not to say that setting up a business offshore in some suitable location is not a viable option – it can be for some businesses – but great care will be necessary.

It may be more sensible – if the offshore option is being considered – to utilise a limited company incorporated overseas, but here again it will be crucial to be able to demonstrate that the company is not centrally managed and controlled from the UK and also that it does not have permanent establishment in the UK. Either of these could expose the company to a charge of UK CT.

Summary

All too often business structure is something that happens organically or even accidentally. At best the business will survive through serendipity, at worst it will cause additional tax liabilities and other financial costs which may be unnecessary and could even harm its prospects for survival.

A large number of start-ups don't make it through their first three years. Some of these fail because they don't plan their tax liabilities and others fail because they choose to operate through a business structure which leads to them paying unnecessary amounts of tax.

Consider the following questions:

- Do you have choice over the business structure?

- What will be the best business structure for you as an individual?

- What structure will best suit your type of business?

- Will a partnership be suitable? Who can you have as partners? Is a family partnership a good idea or are there other types of partnership that might be suitable?

- When will the first tax bills be due under the various structures, how much will they be and when will subsequent annual bills be due?

- Will your customers prefer you to operate through a limited company?

- Will your investors prefer you to operate through a limited company?

- Which structure will best suit the assets you have and how you would prefer to own them?

- As the business grows will the structure you choose remain suitable and flexible enough; can it be altered easily?

2. Tax Incentives when Starting a Business

Introduction

When starting a new business you will probably need all the financial help you can get. You will not want to be paying more for the essential plant and machinery than you need to and it may be possible to get tax relief on the costs of borrowed money. Such tax reliefs will reduce the costs you incur when starting out, so it is important to make the most of what is available.

The UK tax system offers some specific fiscal incentives and tax reliefs for particular types of business investments in equipment and capital goods of certain categories defined by law. Some things qualify for tax relief whilst others do not. Making sure that you buy the right type of machinery, vehicles or general plant can be the difference between paying full cost and effectively reducing the cost of such expenditures very considerably indeed.

" The UK tax system offers some specific fiscal incentives and tax reliefs for particular types of investments in equipment and capital goods of certain categories. "

There are also specific tax reliefs available for special expenses such as qualifying research and development (R&D) costs, loan finance interest expenses, and even in some circumstances relief for costs you might incur before the business actually starts up. Knowing how this tax relief regime works for you and what deductions are available from it can help you make the right decisions when you are planning what essential plant items to buy and what sort of outside investors you are looking for.

Tax relief can also be available for outside investors in your business if it is structured in specific ways. Whilst these are not always the easiest of tax reliefs to access (successive governments seem to regard any sort of tax relief for business investments as a potential source of tax avoidance abuse by the minority), they can provide real help if you are looking for venture capital assistance and need to give investors an incentive to come on board.

This chapter identifies the main tax reliefs available for the costs you will almost certainly have to incur when starting up in business, and the types of investment in a business that attract tax relief for the outside investors you may be looking to for financial help.

Capital depreciation allowances

The UK's tax regime adopts a rather peculiar stance towards depreciation charges in the P&L account in that it does not allow them as a tax deduction. Despite the fact that depreciation is clearly a genuine business cost – plant does not last forever and has to be replaced so it is legitimate to reflect that wear and tear as a commercial business cost in your profit and loss (P&L) account – the UK tax authorities clearly do not trust accountants to use the *appropriate rate* of depreciation.

The business tax regime therefore stipulates that any commercial depreciation charged in the P&L account (with a few specific exceptions) must be disallowed in the calculation of taxable profits. However, the tax regime then provides for a whole range of specified rates of tax depreciation allowances, known generically as *capital allowances*, which the business may then deduct in computing its taxable profits.

Unfortunately the official capital allowances are not always as generous as the rates of depreciation charged in the financial accounts. On the other hand, in some cases of especially tax-favoured expenditures, more relief is given up front than would be able to be claimed through the P&L account. Hence we frequently end up with a situation where tax relief is given more slowly or more quickly than the deprecation charged in a P&L account, and this results in the tax value of an item of plant being significantly different from its accounting book value. In limited company accounts this can result in a provision having to be made for a complex charge called *deferred taxation*, which is simply the result of the differential rates of deprecation used for taxation and accounting purposes.

The important point for most businesses to bear in mind is that they should maximise their access to tax reliefs on their purchases of equipment, vehicles, plant and machinery, and any other capital items bought for business use. This is why it is important to have a clear understanding of the rates of tax relief that are available for different sorts of expenditure. Failing to understand what is on offer means you may pay more tax on your business profits than is necessary.

Entitlement to capital allowances on plant and machinery

Capital allowances law sets out some basic conditions that have to be met:

- The costs have to be capital in nature – the business must be acquiring something new and of enduring benefit to the activities it is carrying on.

- The costs must be incurred *wholly and exclusively* for business purposes. This is mainly of relevance in the unincorporated business sphere where relief will be denied if a cost is incurred for non-business (private) reasons. HMRC will, however, allow annual tax depreciation allowances for plant used privately to some extent, provided an adjustment for the private use element is made in the annual tax calculations of the unincorporated business.

- The costs must be incurred on the purchase of plant and machinery. This point may seem obvious but it has been the subject of numerous disputes between businesses and HMRC over the years, resulting in many court judgments. When anything novel or unusual comes along which a business is going to use in its trading activities, it will want to claim it as plant and equipment, apparatus or something similar. The tax inspector is tasked with deciding whether the claim is legitimate and whether or not the new item actually comes within the definition of plant and machinery. In some cases this is not straightforward.

What is wholly and exclusively?

A concept that recurs throughout this book and which is key to much tax relief across a variety of areas such as expenses, finance costs and capital expenditures, is the wholly and exclusively provision. It is important to understand that tax law, whether in statute or case law judgements, restricts tax relief where it can be shown that a particular expense has a dual purpose or a non-business motive.

Where it is clear that an expense is incurred primarily for a business purposes – if it is wholly and exclusively a business expense – then there should not be a problem in deducting it as an expense in the business accounts, even if there is some purely incidental private benefit to the proprietor of the business from the expense. If, however, an expense is incurred primarily for a non-business motive, then identifying some incidental business benefit will not be enough to qualify that expense as deductible in computing the taxable profits of the business.

For most equipment purchases it is normally relatively easy to decide if something is plant or machinery, and thus whether it qualifies for tax capital allowances, but this is not always the case.

Machinery and plant has certain key characteristics: it functions, it applies power or movement to something or converts raw materials into something else. It is not merely static and does not simply provide comfort or shelter – rather it is carrying out some important activity as part of the selling or delivery mechanism or services that the business offers to its customers. Businesses should consider what function their items of apparatus or equipment perform as part of the selling or delivery mechanism for the products or services they provide. These are key features of plant and machinery.

It has been in the definition of the small and seemingly innocuous word *plant* that most contentious disputes have arisen, especially in the area of large structures and special purpose buildings, and also in the area of embellishments to buildings, decoration and internal furnishings. Plant is not the building, premises or setting on which or within which a trade or business activity is carried out, rather it is the very thing *with which* the activity is carried out. Buildings and structures will not normally qualify as plant

> " Plant is not the building, premises or setting on which or within which a trade or business activity is carried out, rather it is the very thing with which the activity is carried out. **"**

as they are prohibited from doing so by a specific piece of tax law, unless they are a special purpose building or structure that has been the subject of a tax case judgment at some stage in the past, or it can be shown that the buildings do themselves function specifically as plant and / or machinery.

The key to successful claims by a business to capital allowances reliefs for tax purposes is often to be found in clear cost allocations and apportionments. Where there may be disputes about whether or not something will qualify as plant it will be of great importance that all individual and separate items of costs can be apportioned accurately so that any non-qualifying items which are not plant can be separated out from the qualifying items.

100% tax relief on specific energy-saving business equipment

Some types of plant and equipment currently qualify for 100% tax relief against business profits. Whilst there is currently no general 100% upfront allowance as there has been in the past (except under the annual investment allowance – see below), there is a 100% tax relief available for plant and equipment that is defined as energy efficient.

Where a purchased item comes within certain specific categories as laid down by the Department of Trade and Industry then 100% First Year Allowances (FYA) can be available against a business' taxable profits. There are currently 15 designated technologies and 54 sub-technologies that comprise the Enhanced Capital Allowance (ECA) scheme and these specify which items qualify for 100% tax relief.

Qualifying technologies range from specified boilers, heating and power plants, ventilation and refrigeration equipment, through to certain compressors and lighting equipment. The range of qualifying technologies also includes water-efficient plant and other environmentally friendly plant items as part of the government's avowed policy of encouraging businesses to incur expenditure in a manner which helps it to meet the UK's internationally agreed carbon reduction targets. For complete details and instructions on how to make a claim, follow the instructions on the ECA's website (**www.eca.gov.uk/etl**).

The technology lists are quite extensive and make it clear just how much tax relief can be available; it is always worthwhile making sure you are buying something that qualifies for the maximum rate of tax relief possible.

In some cases establishing entitlement to ECA tax reliefs may even result in your business obtaining a tax refund without actually having paid any tax. Where the business makes a loss and that loss is attributable to these special tax reliefs then this loss can, subject to certain conditions, be surrendered to the HMRC and they will pay a tax credit refund of up to 19% of the loss. For a start-up venture with cash flow concerns this can represent a very important extra source of financial assistance.

Annual investment allowances (AIA)

Tax relief of 100% is also currently available for any business which makes purchases of qualifying plant and machinery up to an amount of £100,000 in any one year. This is in addition to the 100% relief available under the ECA rules mentioned above. This relief is, however, to be scaled down to only £25,000 from April 2012.

Thus plant and equipment which does not qualify as energy efficient may still attract 100% tax relief if it is below the £100,000 cost threshold. Clearly for large businesses this is of minimal use, but for start-ups this represents a very important tax relief and will make a significant contribution to reduction in the tax liabilities of the early years. A new business spending £200,000 on plant and equipment, of which £100,000 qualifies as energy efficient technologies, will still be able to obtain 100% upfront tax relief on all its costs in this area.

First Year Allowances – temporary tax reliefs

At different times over the years – for example to provide assistance to businesses incurring expensive investment costs on plant and machinery in times of economic stringency – governments have offered a first year allowance

(FYA) to businesses for their qualifying investment in plant and machinery, with rates varying from 30% to 100%. An example of how FYAs might be used by governments came during the 2007-2009 recession, when up to the period ending 31 March 2010 a 40% FYA was in force to provide some economic assistance. A machine costing £100,000 would have attracted £40,000 relief against business profits under these rules.

Not all equipment purchases will qualify for FYAs at times when they are made available. Some types of expenditure are specifically excluded, for example motor cars, plant for hiring out to customers, plant for leasing overseas and any plant purchased by an unincorporated business which is subject to private use by the proprietor. Generally, though, most types of plant costs will qualify for the rate of available FYA and will also include the costs of purchasing, moving and installing the plant or equipment, together with any incidental costs of the purchase, such as professional fees. Costs of demolishing old plant and removing it from the site can also be regarded as qualifying plant costs for these purposes.

Annual writing down allowances

Annual capital allowances are generally given on a reducing balance basis. Thus £100,000 will attract a 20% allowance in year one and the remaining £80,000 will attract an allowance of £16,000 in year two and so on. As mentioned above, if a special FYA is available then the allowance in year one could be between 30% and 100%.

The costs of plant and machinery which are not written off against taxable profits in one year are carried forward to the subsequent tax period as *tax written-down values*. They can then be depreciated against taxable profits in that subsequent accounting year or period at an annual rate specified in the tax regulations. This is currently set at an annual writing down allowance of 20%.

Thus if a business purchases plant costing £100,000 at a time when FYAs are being offered by the government, it will receive a 40% FYA and carry forward £60,000 written down values on that plant expenditure to its subsequent tax period. In that next period it can claim a profits deduction of 20% against this amount (£12,000) and can do the same against the profits of future years. It is clear that at an annual rate of 20% on a reducing balance basis it actually takes a long time to write off 100% of the real costs of an item of plant and machinery against profits.

Plant and machinery bought by a business is generally regarded as added to and sold from a single general *pool* so that all purchases and sales are dealt with as forming part of a single growing and diminishing plant and machinery category. This is not always the case and specific types of plant and machinery are kept separate from the general pool (more detail on this is given later in the chapter).

If an item of plant is bought for £100,000 and depreciated for three years at 20% the tax deductible amounts each year would be as shown in Table 2.1 (assuming there is no FYA available this year).

Table 2.1: an item of plant bought for £100,000 and depreciated for three years at 20% (there is no FYA available for the purposes of this example)

Cost	£100,000
20% allowance year 1	(£20,000)
Carried forward	£80,000
20% year 2	(£16,000)
Carried forward	£64,000
20% allowance year 3	(£12,800)
Residue	£51,200

Any plant disposals have to be brought into these capital allowances computations each year as well. Thus if an item of plant is bought for £100,000 and depreciated for two years at 20%, and then sold for £50,000, the computations of the tax deductible amounts each year – where FYA at 40% is also available – would appear as in Table 2.2. In this accounting period the computations would be revised and would produce a single balancing charge in year three on the pool of expenditure.

Table 2.2: an item of plant bought for £100,000 and depreciated for two years at 20% before being sold for £50,000. Here a first year allowance (FYA) of 40% is available.

Costs	£100,000
40% FYA in year 1	(£40,000)
Carried forward to year 2	£60,000
20% allowance in year 2	(£12,000)
Carried forward to year 3	£48,000
Sale proceeds in year 3	(£50,000)
Balancing charge in year 3	(£2,000)
20% year 3	(NIL)
Carried forward	NIL

Special rate costs: long-life assets and integral features

Certain types of capital expenditures are relieved for taxation purposes at a much slower annual depreciation rate of 10%. This rate is essentially reserved for items that HMRC has decided have a much longer useful economic life than normal plant items, and as such will probably be depreciated commercially over a much longer period, generally in excess of 25 years.

These items therefore attract only a 10% annual *deprecation* rate for capital allowances and have to be kept separate from all other items of plant.

The two main categories which fall into this *special rate* expenses pool are items known as *long-life assets* and *integral features*.

Long-life assets

A long-life asset is an item of plant and machinery that has an *expected useful economic life, when new,* of more than 25 years. This was originally intended to apply to large items of plant and equipment or to single large plant installations that will have a very extended useful commercial life and will hence probably be financed and depreciated over a much longer period than is the case for normal items of other plant and machinery.

Clearly if you are buying such large plant items for your business and obtaining tax allowances quickly is important, then you would be well advised to ensure that wherever possible you can demonstrate clearly that the expected useful economic life is going to be below the threshold of 25 years. A key feature here will often be whether or not any item of plant installation has planned maintenance periods or whether specific parts or sub-assemblies need to be replaced at shorter time intervals. This is often the case with very large plant items, and it may well be relatively straightforward to demonstrate that whilst a single plant installation might well be around for a very long time indeed, specific major component parts will not be and hence can be treated as shorter life assets eligible for the normal 20% per annum allowances rather than having to be included in the slower rate of depreciation offered by the Special Rate 10% Pool.

Integral features

HMRC's published guidance on the *integral features* in the buildings class of plant and machinery indicates that the following mainly systemic categories are the only items that they consider are to be included in this 10% special rate pool:

- Electrical systems (including lighting systems).

- Cold water systems.

- Space or water heating systems, powered systems of ventilation, air cooling or air purification, and any floor or ceiling comprised in such systems.

- Lifts, escalators, and moving walkways.

- External solar shading.

When a business is buying, building or refurbishing any premises it will be important to obtain detailed cost allocations and apportionments of the expenditures to enable the identification of these items. Traditionally the integral electrical circuitry and wiring and background lighting in a building did not qualify for any allowances. It does under the integral features provisions, so it is important to ensure that the amount spent on these items is separately identified by the builder, quantity surveyor or architect in any project. Failure to do this will mean the business will not get the correct tax reliefs.

Short-life assets

A special tax relief regime is available for plant and machinery that has an expected life of less than five years. Provided the business keeps accurate and detailed records of such items, a separate pool can be established for them and when they are scrapped or sold within the five-year period a one-off balancing allowance of any unused residues of expenditure is then written off against the taxable profits of the business in one go.

This will normally result in acceleration of the capital expenditure reliefs on such items. Therefore, desktop computers, office furniture and the like should definitely not be overlooked for inclusion in this special sub-category as a tax planning option.

Vehicles

Business vehicles are plant and machinery too but they don't always attract the same rates of capital allowances as other items. Motor cars have historically been treated less generously than other plant items.

Currently the tax depreciation allowances for cars bought for a business are determined according to the carbon dioxide emissions rating of the individual vehicle:

- Cars emitting in excess of 160g/km are put into the special rate pool and attract only a 10% depreciation allowance per annum.

- Cars emitting below this level go into the general plant and machinery pool where they attract the normal 20% per annum rate of allowance.

- Cars emitting below 110g/km may qualify for a 100% deduction against business profits provided they are not subject to any private use by the proprietor of an unincorporated business.

- Similarly cars and vans with no emissions (broadly electric vehicles), will also qualify for this 100% deduction against taxable profits unless there is private use by the proprietor of an unincorporated business.

Cars purchased by unincorporated sole traders and partnerships for the purposes of their business will generally be subject to private use by the proprietors. Such vehicles have to be kept separate from the general pool and each is treated as a single car pool with the annual writing down allowances subject to a restriction for private use, which has to be included on a self-assessment computation when submitted to the HMRC.

Owners of unincorporated businesses also need to be aware that purchases of very expensive vehicles can occasionally attract the attention of their inspector of taxes, who may argue that the costs should be restricted not only for private use but also for an element of personal choice. This may result in the total cost of the vehicle being reduced by a substantial amount before the starting point for tax allowances is agreed. In practice it is fairly rare for HMRC to do this and they will usually only take such action for the most expensive luxury cars.

Computer software

Special tax depreciation allowances are available for the costs of purchasing or otherwise dealing with computer software. Generally a separate pool is established that receives a 20% per annum writing-down allowance. Such expenditures can also attract the 100% AIA mentioned earlier.

Computer software costs may be classified in some cases as intangible expenses and then attract tax relief under the special regime for intangible assets if the expense is incurred by a limited company (more detail on this later).

Much of the cost of computer software can be regarded as a relatively short-term expense. The costs of renewing annual software licenses and keeping a website up-to-date can generally be regarded as normal P&L costs and expensed there rather than treated as eligible for slower capital allowances. Upfront costs of setting up a website and obtaining an initial license to use software will have to be regarded as capital expenses and should be included in the software pool for the purposes of capital allowances.

Capital allowances for particular business areas

There are some specialist areas of the capital allowances regime that provide for tax relief on certain costs incurred in particular industries. Shipping, waste disposal, dredging, sports grounds and stadia, mineral extraction and quarrying, are all included in this category and if your business is one of these areas you may be able to obtain additional capital expenditures reliefs by making the appropriate claim. Allowances are generally at the normal rate of 20% annual allowances with the AIAs discussed above also available in some circumstances.

Research and development costs

Where your business is carrying out research into a new product or service it may qualify for special tax reliefs if you can demonstrate that the type of costs you are incurring qualify as research and development (R&D). This is a special category of business expenses which is currently deemed politically deserving of additional tax relief assistance. Normal R&D costs can attract 100% relief against business profits and a small business (as defined by HMRC) may qualify for an extra 75% relief, so these allowances are well worth following up.

However, it is critical to note that these R&D allowances are only currently available to limited companies and not to unincorporated businesses. Thus if your business is about to embark on a very extensive and expensive research and development project, or you are setting up a new venture to exploit an innovative product or service idea and this relief is going to be an

> **Normal R&D costs can attract 100% relief against business profits and a small business may qualify for an extra 75% relief. However, these R&D allowances are only currently available to limited companies.**

important cost element, then your choice of business structure is likely to be heavily influenced by the availability of this tax deduction.

R&D allowances will only be available when the detailed qualification criteria for what qualifies for this special relief are met and specialist advice is probably advisable if your business is looking to pursue this relief, but do not be discouraged. Where a business is embarking on an innovative and systematic programme of research towards developing a new idea or product, it may well be worthwhile exploring this further. For new business start-ups this relief can be especially beneficial if there is going to be a significant lead time before the business starts to turn a profit.

Tax credit relief can even result in HMRC making tax credit repayments to a business. In these circumstances you surrender your early years losses arising as a result of these costs to the HMRC, and they send the business a cheque for 14% of the loss. This can represent very useful cash flow assistance.

Intangibles and goodwill

If you are buying a business rather than starting from scratch you may have the opportunity to purchase the goodwill from the vendor. Companies get tax relief on the costs of purchased goodwill, unincorporated business do not. Thus if this is going to be a significant business start-up cost you may wish to choose a limited company structure for the new venture specifically in order to get tax relief on this expense.

Another reason for allocating some of the purchase costs of a business venture to goodwill is that this element of the purchase price does not normally carry a Stamp Duty Land Tax liability, whereas property costs do once the base threshold of £150,000 is exceeded.

Tax relief against company profits is also available on the costs of buying or generating *intangibles* internally. This may be intellectual property or similar costs such as brands or goodwill. Tax relief here is given in accordance with Generally Accepted

> **"** Depreciation on goodwill (technically referred to as amortisation) is an allowable P&L deduction and is one of the few types of depreciation allowed against profits for tax purposes. **"**

Accounting Principles (GAAP). This means that provided an appropriate rate of commercial depreciation is applied to the intangible and can be justified by reference to normal commercial accounting standards, then the commercial depreciation charged in a company's P&L account is simply left as an allowable deduction against profits for tax purposes.

Thus depreciation on goodwill (technically referred to as amortisation) is an allowable P&L deduction and is one of the few types of depreciation allowed against profits for tax purposes. However, if a limited company is preparing its commercial accounts under International Financial Reporting Standards (IFRS) goodwill is no longer amortised; it is revalued every year and the amount of any resulting impairment will be written off as a cost against profits. It would still be amortised where UK commercial accounting standards are used.

There are alternative and differing types of tax relief, akin to capital allowances, for expenses of other types of intangibles such as buying patents and know-how, under which capital allowances at the normal 20% pool rate are allowed, rather than commercial depreciation.

Allowances for renovating premises

When your business acquires new premises from which to trade, especially when you are just starting out, it is almost inevitable that you will need to spend money getting the place ready for use. This will be the case whether it is a retail shop or showroom, offices, or a workshop or factory.

This is an important pre-planning issue and getting tax relief for these costs can be a tricky problem. HMRC attitudes here are to some extent coloured by 1923 case law, one in particular on an ocean-going steamship which was bought in an unseaworthy state and therefore needed significant repairs to obtain a seaworthiness certificate. The courts decided that the repairs carried out shortly after purchase were actually non-allowable capital costs because they must have been reflected in a much reduced purchase price, and as such were not to be allowed as deductible repair costs against the business profits after acquisition.

HMRC may seek to apply the same argument to newly acquired premises where repairs have been carried out shortly after purchase. Of course some repairs will have been necessary to put right the wear-and-tear of previous years, but the important question is whether the premises are able to be used by the new business for their intended purpose without those repairs. If the premises were not fit for purpose then the repair costs may well have to be re-categorised as capital costs, but if the property could have been used then the costs will not have to be disallowed for tax purposes simply because they were incurred shortly after the property was acquired.

Clearly there is a lot of subjectivity here and if the right amount of tax relief is to be obtained it will be important to demonstrate clearly what sort of expenditures were carried out when the new premises were acquired and the reason for these.

In two specific areas of commercial expenditure up to 100% tax relief may actually be available for the costs of refurbishing qualifying properties. These are:

1. Renovation of derelict business premises in regions of the UK especially nominated as economically disadvantaged areas.

2. Renovation of flats over shops in high streets and similar locations.

If your business is converting flats over shops for rental or you have to refurbish derelict commercial business premises – space that has been empty for more than a year in a qualifying location – then you should investigate these special reliefs. In these cases even capital expenditures can qualify for tax relief directly through the P&L account. Clearly if the business is just starting out this can be an extremely valuable element of the tax reliefs available to you for purchasing second-hand property.

Industrial and agricultural buildings

Historically the UK's tax system has provided tax relief on 100% of the capital costs of constructing qualifying industrial or agricultural buildings. The tax relief was spread over 25 years at a fixed allowance of 4% per annum of the actual costs of constructing or improving a qualifying building. Industrial buildings were defined as mills, factories or similar premises as well as a long list of qualifying undertakings such as storage warehouses, hotels, transport undertakings and other specialised buildings. Agricultural buildings were defined as buildings in use for the purposes of husbandry and the intensive rearing of livestock or fish.

Unfortunately these reliefs are to become a thing of the past as it has been has decided, despite vociferous lobbying, to abolish these reliefs from 31 March 2011 for companies and 5 April 2011 for unincorporated business. This is extremely bad news if your company built a hotel a couple of years ago and based its business plan on getting 100% tax relief for the total costs over the next 25 years. In future any industrial, agriculture or hotel business will need to pay much more attention than ever before to the apportionment of costs when it is incurring large expenditure programmes so as to ensure that it gets the most out of the capital allowances tax relief regime under the various headings of integral features, enhanced capital allowances, and general plant and machinery.

Pre-trading expenses

Tax relief may be available for some expenses incurred by a business even before it actually started as a venture. The tax regime contains special rules for pre-trading expenses reliefs. These provide that expenses incurred prior to the date on which a business actually starts to trade can attract tax relief on start-up if the expenses would have

> **"** The tax regime contains special rules for pre-trading expenses reliefs. These provide that expenses incurred prior to the date on which a business actually starts to trade can attract tax relief on start-up. **"**

qualified for tax relief had the business been trading when they were incurred. Provided the expense was incurred within a seven-year period before commencement of trading, the expense can be included in a list of pre-trading costs to be allowed as deductible expenses on the day the business starts.

For companies the expenses are treated as deductible on day one of its trading period. For the unincorporated business these costs are treated as a pre-trade loss arising in the first tax year a business actually trades.

Venture capital reliefs for investors

There are two main types of structured share investment scheme available for UK investors in small limited company ventures. These are the Enterprise Investment Scheme (EIS) and Venture Capital Trusts (VCT). Both of these offer a limited form of income tax relief for investors in respect of qualifying subscriptions for new shares in qualifying companies. The investor subscribes for shares and gets income tax relief against their normal tax liabilities at a specified rate for the amount of their investment.

Thus if you are looking to raise significant venture capital for your business venture and it is *business angel* investors you are looking to attract, this may be the sort of company share structure to use. It is important to recognise from the outset that these sort of structured and tax relievable investments are only available where a venture capitalist subscribes for new shares in a business venture being run as a limited company. There is no equivalent tax relief available for similar investments in unincorporated businesses ventures.

Enterprise Investment Scheme (EIS) shares

An individual can get 20% income tax relief against their general income tax liability under this scheme for subscribing for qualifying shares in single qualifying companies. There is a maximum relief amount of shares subscribed for of £500,000 and a minimum of £500.

There are some fairly rigorous rules about the types of trade or businesses which the investee company may or may not be involved in, in order for the shares subscribed for to qualify for this relief.

Additionally the company must carry on the trade activity for a minimum period of three years after receiving the share subscriptions, during which no disqualifying events must take place, such as a cessation of trading or the investor becoming connected with the company. An investor who is connected to the company in various ways, for example as a prior shareholder, director or employee, cannot normally qualify for this relief.

If you are looking to raise capital in this way, specialist advice will be needed to ensure that your company meets all the qualifying conditions imposed by the relevant tax laws. Meeting the numerous anti-avoidance conditions can be onerous, but EIS reliefs can prove a very useful source of finance. It may be easier to convince an investor to put their money into the business if they are going to get 20% income tax relief.

An additional CGT deferral may also be available for investors in EIS shares, enabling them to delay payment of personal CGT bills. This can prove another valuable means of attracting would-be investors.

Venture Capital Trusts (VCT)

Venture Capital Trusts are essentially quoted companies which invest in a range of EIS businesses by taking shares in them – this is another venture capital tax relief available for those who wish to spread risks even further.

The investor here will obtain 30% income tax relief on their subscriptions for units in the VCT, which then invest these funds in the new businesses. It may not be an easy task to persuade venture capitalists to invest their capital in your business, but if the investor is going to obtain significant tax reliefs this may be an incentive for them to do so.

There are restrictions on the time periods for which the investor must hold their shares and there is currently a maximum amount of £200,000 they can invest in the trust.

Tax relief for borrowing costs

Almost all businesses have to borrow funds at some stage, especially at the start. It will be of crucial importance that you get tax relief on the costs of funding these borrowings.

Where the business itself pays interest on borrowed money, for example the overdraft or loan interest, then those costs can be deducted directly against the profits of the business as a genuine cost of running the enterprise. The only criteria, which is mainly of relevance to the unincorporated business, is that the interest charges must be incurred wholly and exclusively for the purposes of the trade. This means that where the interest arises directly from borrowings used to fund business expenditure, there should be no problem.

However, if, for example, the proprietor of a guesthouse which is also their own home borrows money to finance the purchase then interest relief will have to be restricted to that part of the loan which financed the business proportion of the property. No tax relief will be available against the interest on that part of the loan which financed the acquisition of their private accommodation. Clearly there is often going to be an element of judgement here and the final allowance may have to be the subject of negotiation with the inspector of taxes.

Tax relief for interest charges may also be restricted where the proprietor of a business overdraws their personal capital account with the business. In this situation HMRC can argue that the interest charges arise for personal reasons and do not wholly and exclusively arise from the costs of running the business. In this situation some of the interest may have to be disallowed for tax purposes.

Normally the incidental costs of obtaining, negotiating and renewing loan finance or business financial and overdraft arrangements will attract full tax relief against profits.

There are other forms of loan arrangement and finance costs which can also attract tax relief for their interest costs. Where an individual borrows money personally, outside of a business, to lend to a business carrying on a trade or to invest as capital in a business carrying on a trade, this interest will attract tax relief against their general income. Similarly, where an individual borrows money to buy shares in a close company – a small family company controlled by five or fewer shareholders or by any number of directors – the interest thereon will also attract income tax relief against their general income.

Loss reliefs on start-ups

When a business commences it is not unusual for losses to arise in the early years. This tends to be the period when marketing and advertising costs are highest and when various costs have to be incurred just to get the business going, with little return for quite some time. Some businesses inevitably have a long lead time to success and thus trading losses may well be incurred.

The tax regime provides some special reliefs for start-up losses, particularly in the area of income tax. The most important criteria is to be able to demonstrate from the outset that the losses arise from a genuine commercially-inspired business venture.

Tax law contains anti-avoidance provisions aimed at preventing the individual structuring their activities so as to obtain tax loss relief (and possibly income tax refunds) in respect of what might be termed *hobby* losses; a business run for personal amusement, gratification or out of admiration for a family member might fail this test. Lack of success need not mean that a business activity is not commercially inspired though, because failure does not indicate lack of commercial inspiration.

It is often difficult to tell where a hobby ends and a commercial venture begins – many hobbies start off in a fairly small way and gradually grow into a successful business venture. One tempting suggestion might be to argue that the hobby stops and the commercially inspired business begins when profits first arise; I have seen this argument put by a tax inspector myself. This need not be the case. A more accurate definition is that a taxable business begins when a business organises itself on a commercial basis and sets out to make a profit, and more importantly when relief for the losses it makes potentially becomes available against the individual's other taxable income, if they have any.

In the first four tax years of an unincorporated business' existence, any tax losses which arise can be *carried back* and relieved against other taxable earnings which the individual incurring the loss had in the previous three tax years prior to the year of loss. This may mean that tax liabilities paid on salary or other income during those years can be clawed back as a useful cash flow bonus to the business in its formative and costly early years. Any losses not utilised in this manner can be carried forward and used against future years' profits arising from the same trade carried on by the business.

Sideways loss relief may also be available against an individual's general income in the year of an income tax loss incurred in running a business, although in the early years the carry back option identified above is probably preferable.

When you start your business the choice of your first accounting date can be critical to your ability to access loss relief in the early years. Setting your accounting date as the 5 April is probably the best choice as it will allow you to access these early years loss relief provisions as fast as possible and thus get any available tax refunds from other earlier years' earnings as quickly as possible.

> **" A taxable business begins when a business organises itself on a commercial basis and sets out to make a profit, and more importantly when relief for the losses it makes potentially becomes available against the individual's other taxable income, if they have any. "**

This is one of the first things you should discuss with your accountant if you appoint one to advise on your business activities. He may well choose an accounting date for you and his choice may be affected by any number of factors, only one of which might be your ability to access loss reliefs. Make sure that you have a direct input on this choice.

Summary

The early years of a business are always expensive and usually entail a lot of investment and fundraising. This chapter has covered some of the costs which attract tax relief and some of the ways in which investors can get tax incentives for investing in your business. In summary, these are:

- Qualifying plant and machinery purchases will normally attract a 20% tax deduction annually against business profits.

- Currently a 100% allowance is available for the first £100,000 of business expenditure on qualifying plant and machinery.

- Plant and machinery generally covers all business equipment and apparatus, and may also include unusual items if HMRC will accept that they come within the technical definitions. Disputed items may sometimes have to be decided by the courts if agreement on their qualifying status cannot be reached with HMRC.

- Some special types of plant and machinery, for example energy efficient items, can attract a deduction of 100% of their costs against business profits.

- Restrictions to the tax allowances available can apply to business vehicles depending upon the level of their carbon dioxide emissions.

- Some types of fixtures and fittings, known as integral features, in a building and other long-lasting items will attract tax allowances at a slower 10% per annum rate to reflect their slower depreciation.

- Short-life assets – those with a life of less than five years – will attract faster tax allowances to reflect their shorter expected useful life in the business.

- Companies may also qualify for enhanced capital allowances on research and development (R&D) costs and the costs of intangibles such as intellectual property.

- Where a corporate business incurs revenue expenses on R&D it may also be able to claim enhanced tax credits for these costs of up to 175%.

- There are also some special allowances for particular trades such as mining and quarrying, and the costs of renovating business premises in designated regions of the UK.

- Investors in specially defined companies may be able to claim income tax relief on the acquisition of shares in these companies under special schemes such as the Enterprise Investment Scheme or via investments in Venture Capital Trusts.

- A business which incurs losses in its early years may be entitled to carry those losses forward against future business profits or possibly (for unincorporated businesses), claim backwards relief against the business owner's personal income of prior years.

- Tax relief should also be available against profits for the interest costs of business borrowings on funds to start up.

3. The Tax Stages of a Business

Introduction

All businesses have tax obligations to meet when they commence trading. Getting this wrong can lead to problems with the tax authorities and cause potentially serious financial difficulties. Getting it right means that you may pay less tax than you otherwise would, and that you pay your tax liabilities at the right time – not too early and not too late.

Getting it right also creates the right impression with the HMRC. Tax enquiries (known by HMRC as Compliance Checks), particularly those on businesses, are conducted largely on the basis of risk assessment. A business that has a good track record and indicates clearly by the way it interacts with the tax authorities that it is controlling its tax liabilities well, attending to its payment and filing tax obligations properly

> **"** You should regard HMRC in the same way as any other supplier or creditor that your business has to deal with; debts owing to them need to be managed and controlled, especially as tax is likely to be one of the largest liabilities of a business, **"**

and on time, will inevitably be accorded a lower risk rating than those who do not. Your objective should be to secure as low a risk rating for your business and its tax affairs as you can. These obligations, though somewhat time consuming, need not be too onerous if approached as just another business administration function.

The most important rule for any business dealing with its creditors is of course to keep in contact; creditors must be informed of what is going on at all stages. You should regard HMRC in the same way as any other supplier or creditor that your business has to deal with; debts owing to them need to be managed and controlled, especially as tax is likely to be one of your largest liabilities, and so represents a major cash flow item at certain times of the year. This means informing HMRC in good time of the commencement of the business, prompt payment of tax, PAYE, NICs, etc., and keeping in touch with them when returns and other official documents are due to be filed.

Starting up – income tax rules

Sole traders and partnerships are liable to income tax on their business profits and also have some NICs to pay as well. Depending on their current and expected level of turnover a business may also have to register for VAT.

It is therefore important to understand the particular rules which apply for the assessment of income tax when your business starts to trade. These are not always straightforward and at times can seem unnecessarily complicated. The rules which apply to your business will determine how soon you have to pay your first income tax liabilities.

Anyone liable to income tax has to provide HMRC with a self-assessment statement or tax return form for each tax year. This has to include a statement of the taxable profits from their business, prepared according to normal commercial accounting principles. Most businesses of any size will appoint an accountant to do this for them, although this is not a legal obligation.

Accounting date

The profits disclosed in a business' accounts have to be assessed for specified *basis periods* and income tax years. These do not always coincide. The business has to provide HMRC with a profit figure to be assessed for each tax year that it is in existence. Over the entire lifespan of the business the profits assessed to income tax will be equal to the profits the business actually earns, but at the start there may be some mismatch. This will depend upon the accounting date you choose. There is no obligation to choose any particular date but it will affect how the profits liable to income tax are assessed and when.

Basis periods and tax assessments

The way your profits will be assessed to income tax is best illustrated by examples. The basic rule is that there has to be an amount of profit assessed for each tax year in which your business is in existence.

Profits are assessed according to the 12-month annual accounting period you choose to use, and the amount assessed for each tax year is normally the profit for the 12-month accounting period ending in the tax year.

For example, profits for the 12 months to 31 August 2009 would normally form the basis of the 2009/2010 assessable amount. Thus if the business starts up on 1 January 2010 there has to be a tax assessable amount for the tax year 2009/2010 and every tax year for which the business trades thereafter until it ceases.

Example 1

Jonathan starts to trade as a freelance sound engineering consultant on 1 January 2010 and his accounts are made up for 12 months to 31 December 2010. Profits for that period are £36,000. The assessments will be as follows:

2009/2010	Period assessed: 1/1/2010 to 5/4/2010
	Profits assessed: 95/365 x £36,000 = £9,370
2010/2011	Period assessed: 1/1/2010 to 31/12/2010
	Profits assessed: £36,000

The tax year 2011/2012 will be assessed on the profits of the 12 months to the next year end on 31 December 2011.

Example 1 shows that the profits of the period 1 January 2010 to 5 April 2010 (a 95-day period) have been taxed twice in the first two tax years of the business' existence. This is not a mistake! It is an inevitable consequence of the rule that says a business must have a tax assessment for each year in which it trades.

This profit assessed twice is known as *overlap profit* and in the above example it is £9,370. This amount is carried forward until the business ceases and is deducted from the profits assessable for that year, so that the amount of profits assessed over the life of the business equal the profits actually made.

A business can also trigger access to this *overlap relief* on some occasions by changing its accounting date. There are special rules that limit when and how often a business is permitted to change its accounting date, but this can be an opportunity to reduce one year's profits substantially by accessing the brought forward overlap relief before cessation. An example of when this might be done is when profits are rising rapidly and deferring payment of rising tax liabilities will be beneficial.

A business would do this by perhaps extending its accounting period by six months so that extra profits are included in the amount that will be assessed for income tax, but this would enable the business to use up some of its overlap relief and this might in some instances result in a lower overall taxable profit for the tax year. For a business with significant overlap profit created on start-up it is always worth bearing this in mind if profits rise or fall rapidly, as this may be the time to consider using your overlap profits.

If you choose 5 April as your annual accounting date this double assessment will not occur and there will then be no overlap profits, as can be seen in Example 2.

Example 2

Casey starts to trade on 1 January 2010 as a freelance criminologist and makes her accounts up to 5 April 2010 earning profits of £12,000, and then again to 5 April 2011 earning £48,000. The tax assessable profits will be:

2009/2010	Period assessed: 1/1/2010 to 5/4/2010
	Profits assessed = £12,000
2010/2011	Period assessed: 6/4/2010 to 5/4/2011
	Profits assessed = £48,000

Example 2 shows there is no double assessed amount of taxable profits and hence no overlap profit and no relief to carry forward against future years.

If a business chooses to make its first accounts up to a date which is shorter than a 12-month period then the same general rules apply about the first tax year and the 12-month period of account for each subsequent tax year. The objective is to establish the ongoing rule that 12 months' profits are assessed for the tax year in which the 12-month accounting period ends.

Example 3

Nicky starts to trade as a freelance photographer on 1 January 2010 and chooses 30 June as her annual accounting date. Profits for the 181-day period to 30 June 2010 are £16,000 and for the next 365 days to 30 June 2011 are £24,000. The assessable profits for her first three tax years in business will be as follows:

For the tax year 2009/2010 Nicky is assessed on 95 days of the 181-day period between 1 January and 30 June 2010. Hence 95/181 x £16,000 = £8,398.

For the tax year 2010/2011 Nicky is assessed on the full 181 days' profits to 30 June 2010 plus 184 days of the profits for the 365-day period to 30 June 2011 to make a total period of 365 days. Hence £16,000 + (184/365 x £24,000) = £28,098.

For the tax year 2011/2012 the normal preceding year basis of assessment is established so Nicky is assessed on the period of 12 months ending in the tax year, i.e. the 365 days to 30 June 2011.

2009/2010	Period assessed: 1/1/2010 to 5/4/2010 (95 days)
	Profits assessed: 95/181 x £16,000 = £8,398
2010/2011	Period assessed: 1/1/2010 to 31/12/2010 (365 days)
	Profits assessed: £16,000 + (184/365 x £24,000) = £16,000 + £12,098 = £28,098
2011/2012	Period assessed: 1/7/2010 to 30/6/2011 (365 days)
	Profits assessed = £24,000

Thus it can be seen that the profits for the period to 5 April 2010 (£8,398) have been assessed for both 2009/10 and 2010/11. Similarly the profits for the period 1 July 2010 to 31 December 2010 (£12,098) have been assessed in both the 2010/2011 year and the 2011/2012 year.

Thus Nicky has overlap profits to carry forward as overlap relief totalling £20,497. This is calculated as follows:

Overlap profits = £8,398 (95-day period 1/1/10 to 5/4/10) + £12,098 (184-day period 1/7/10 to 31/12/10).

This overlap relief will be carried forward and deducted from the tax assessable profits for the tax year in which Nicky's business ceases.

Choosing an accounting date

The choice of an accounting date can affect two important aspects of tax compliance:

1. The time lag between earning profits and paying the tax on those profits, and

2. The time lag between the end of the business' financial accounting period and having to get the books and records for that period up-to-date so that the profits can be entered on the tax return.

As mentioned above the normal rule is that profits of a 12-month period ending in the tax year form the basis period for the self-assessment for that tax year. Thus the year to 31 July 2011 will form the basis period for the tax self-assessment for the tax year 2011/2012.

The balancing payment for the tax liability on profits of the year to 31 July 2011 must be paid on or before 31 January 2013, thus giving 18 months between the end of the accounting period and the payment of the final tax liability for that period. The tax return for 2011/12 also has to be in to HMRC by this same date.

> **An accounting date early in the tax year arguably gives the longest time delay for the preparation of a business' accounts and the payment of its tax liabilities.**

If the accounting date chosen by the business was 31 March 2011, the period of 12 months' profits as shown by the accounts would be assessed for tax year 2010/2011 and the tax return and balancing payment would then fall due a year earlier on 31 January 2012, representing a time delay of only nine months.

So an accounting date early in the tax year arguably gives the longest time delay for the preparation of a business' accounts and the payment of its tax liabilities. Using an accounting date of 30 April 2010, for example, would give a lead time of 21 months from the end of the accounting date to the time when the balancing tax payment has to be made on 31 January 2012 and the tax return covering those profits has to be submitted.

However, this is not always an advisable tactic because it would mean that the tax liability payments would always be lagging one year behind the accounting periods. This might be fine for a business where profits are relatively stable or perhaps rising steadily; the tax bills being paid would always be lower than those due on the current profits. But for a business with profits that fluctuate considerably from year-to-year – property development for example – this could mean that in some years the business would be paying tax bills on last year's high profits when in the current year they have low profits and reduced cash flow.

Unless the business is very good at providing for tax bills in advance, as the years go by this can lead to significant cash flow problems. For this reason many businesses and their accountants prefer to use either 31 March or 5 April as the income tax accounting date so that the tax bills tend to fluctuate fairly closely in line with their current year's profits.

Cessation

When an income tax business ceases, its final tax assessment is on the profits of the period from the end of its last basis period to the date of cessation. Any overlap relief is deducted at this time. For an example of how this works in practice see Example 4.

Example 4

Joshua has been trading for many years as a self-employed fisherman but decides to close his business down on 31 March 2012. He has used 31 December annually as his accounting date. He has overlap profit brought forward of £14,000, his profits to 31 December 2011 are £40,000 and profits for the period to cessation on 31 March 2012 are £22,000.

The tax assessment for the final year of the business' existence, 2011/2012, is £62,000 less the overlap relief of £14,000 = £48,000.

National Insurance (NI)

When someone starts up as self-employed they will normally have two types of National Insurance contributions (NICs) to pay. The first is class 2 and this is payable monthly by direct debit. The current rate for the self-employed is £2.40 per week and when an individual starts a business they need to register as self-employed and start paying this on a monthly basis straightaway.

The second type of NICs payable by the self-employed is class 4 and this is payable twice a year in instalments along with the income tax liability in July and January. Class 4 NICs are payable at a rate of 8% between profits of £5,715 and £43,875 per annum and at 1% on assessed profits over this upper threshold (figures for 2010/11 tax year).

Starting up – corporation tax rules

The rules for assessing the taxable profits of companies are much more simple at start-up than those for income tax. A company pays its corporation tax (CT) bills by reference to its chosen company accounting period and the CT rates are set by reference to the fiscal year, which for companies runs from 1 April to 31 March.

A company can make its annual accounts up to any date it chooses, although most have fairly standardised dates (for example 31 March or 31 December). A company can also change its company accounting date, subject to Company Law rules; it can shorten it as many times as it chooses over the years but may only lengthen it once every five years.

When a new company is incorporated HMRC will normally assume that this is the start of its first 12-month CT accounting period (CTAP) and will then expect that the business' first return will be for the 12 months running from that date. In fact this is often not the case because there is frequently a gap between the date of the company's actual incorporation and the date the company subsequently commences in business.

This is effectively a dormant period and need not be the subject of a detailed CT return or the preparation of formalised accounts for submission to HMRC as the company may not be trading or carrying on any business for this period. Alternatively this period can be the subject of the submission of a nil return if the company only starts to carry on any business at a later stage. The date on which the company starts to trade or carry on any active business will be the commencement of its first CTAP, for which a CT return will be needed (Form CT600), so HMRC should be informed from the outset when a company starts to trade.

HMRC can only accept a CT return period of 12 months or shorter and must be notified well in advance of the dates of each relevant return period. They will not accept a CT return for longer than 12 months.

Thus if a company is incorporated on 15 December 2009 and starts to trade on 1 January 2010 it will have a nil CT return to submit for the period 15 December 2009 to 31 December 2009 and then its first full CT return will be for the 12 months from 1 January 2010 to 31 December 2010. If the company makes its first accounts up to 31 March 2010 then its second CT return will be for the period 1 January 2010 to 31 March 2010 and the third return will be for the 12 months 1 April 2010 to 31 March 2011, and so on.

If a company prepares its first accounts for a period of trading for 18 months then it will have to submit CT returns for a 12-month period from the trading start date and then for a six-month period for the rest of that accounting period. If the company prepares its first accounts for six months and then 12 months it will have to submit CT returns for those two separate periods in turn.

When corporation tax will be due

The choice of accounting date will determine when and how soon the CT liability for an accounting period falls due. The date on which your company will have to pay its tax depends upon its size.

Companies with total aggregate profits and capital gains for a 12 month CTAP below £1.5m will pay CT at the small or marginal companies' tax rates, currently 21% for profits or gains below £300,000 with marginal rates applying between £300,000 and £1.5m.

Their CT bills will normally fall due nine months and one day after the end of their CTAP, thus a company with an accounting date of 31 December will have one annual CT payment to make on or before 1 October.

Companies with profits and gains annually in excess of the threshold of £1.5m must pay their CT bills by quarterly instalments. The first instalment is due six months and 13 days from the start of the accounting period and the last instalment is due three months and 14 days from the end of the accounting period, with the other two falling due at equal intervals between these two dates. Thus in any 12-month accounting period a large rate company will make four instalment payments of CT, the first relating to the previous company accounting period and three relating to the current accounting period.

Forming a partnership

Income tax

If a business starts up as a partnership then the income tax rules outlined earlier for the commencing years' assessable profits will apply in the same way. The chief difference will be that each partner will have their own self-assessment on their share of the profits. The partnership will have to submit a partnership tax return showing the allocation of the profits among the partners and this will form the basis of their individual annual tax self-assessments.

If a sole trader takes in a partner so that a new partnership is formed for income tax purposes, then consideration has to be given to the special rules which can apply for income tax on the cessation of a business and the commencement of a business.

Normally where a sole trader takes in a partner this will be treated for them as simply continuing in business for the purposes of income tax, they will not be treated as ceasing the existing business and starting a new one. This is known as *continuation treatment*.

The newly joined partner will be treated as commencing in business and the commencement rules summarised above for income tax start-ups will have to be applied separately to this partner's share of the profits on that commencement as if they were starting their own income tax business. This can be confusing because it can mean that partners can have different income tax basis periods for the same tax year.

Example 5

Tony has been in business for many years as a flying instructor and uses 31 December as his annual accounting date. On 1 October 2010 he takes in a partner, James, to assist in the business with packing parachutes.

Tony's self-assessment for 2010/2011 will be based on his share of the business profits for the year to 31 December 2010.

James will share in those same profits from 1 October 2010 to 31 Dcember 2010. However, his self-assessment for 2010/2011 will be based on his profit-share for the period 1 October 2010 to 5 April 2011.

When preparing the partnership return covering the accounting period to 31 December 2010 an estimate will have to be used of the new partner's profit-share as the result for the period 1 January 2011 to 5 April 2011 will probably not be known yet.

Tony's assessable profits for the next tax year, 2011/2012, will be based on his share of the profits to 31 December 2011, as will James', and so on in future years. James will have overlap profit to carry forward for the period 1 January 2011 to 5 April 2011.

Special rules may also apply for determining the basis periods when businesses merge to form a partnership or where two partnerships are brought together to form a larger business. In such circumstances it is necessary to decide whether the merged partnership can to any extent be regarded as recognisably being the business of either or both of the old partnerships.

If the new business when merged represents a substantively new and different business from either of the old ones then HMRC may contend that both old businesses should be treated as ceasing and restarting as one new business for income tax purposes.

Alternatively, they may contend that this cessation treatment should only be applied to one of the businesses. This may often be the case where a small business is taken over by a much larger one.

To look at it another way, the occasion of one business taking over another, or when two businesses merge, might be an opportunity for one or both to be treated as ceasing and thereby gain access to otherwise unusable overlap relief currently being carried forward. This might facilitate significant reductions in income tax liabilities for one or both of the two businesses being brought together.

The occasion of a partner leaving the partnership will also affect their individual basis periods in the same way as it does an individual sole trader. When a partner leaves a partnership they are treated as ceasing to have a self-employed source of income, and this will trigger their access to any overlap relief brought forward (as illustrated in Example 4 earlier).

Other taxes on partnership start-up

The formation of a partnership can have other tax implications as well. When someone takes in a partner or several individuals to form a new partnership there may be alterations in the ownership of assets such as property or business goodwill. The CGT implications and possibly also stamp duty land tax (SDLT) of such changes will need to be considered.

Capital gains tax (CGT)

If monetary or another valuable consideration changes hands when a new partner is taken into a business then there may well be CGT liabilities to calculate. If a new partner buys into a business then the person selling them their partnership assets or partnership share, or part of it, will have a potential CGT liability to pay to HMRC and this will have to be included on their self-assessment for the relevant tax year.

Capital gains tax liabilities can also arise when partners rearrange their asset-sharing or asset ownership ratios among themselves; for example where three partners owning the business premises equally (each has 33.3%) change things around so that one person has a 50% share and the others now have only 25%. The two individuals who now own 25% have each made a disposal of an 8.3% interest (33.3% - 25% = 8.3%) to the person who now owns 50%. This is a potential occasion of charge to CGT because partners are potentially regarded as connected persons for CGT purposes by HMRC.

However, in most cases where the business partners are not family members HMRC will not invoke the *market value rules* that could mean CGT liabilities might arise on deemed or actual asset disposals amongst the partners. Thus any amounts they actually pay among themselves will normally be used as the figure for computing any CGT liabilities, which may of course be zero. This is because HMRC will assume that non-family related partners are acting *at arm's length* among themselves.

Market value rules

Market value rules may be imposed by HMRC when profit sharing ratios or ownership of shares changes in a partnership. HMRC will examine these transcations to ensure there is not a tax avoidance motive behind them, i.e. the assets or shares must not be bought for less than their market value.

Where the parties are connected and therefore not regarded as acting at arm's length, there is the potential for capital gains to arise, but here a *holdover relief* election can normally be made to defer any such tax liabilities. The effect of this is that the transferee – the person receiving the share of the assets – takes over the transferor's base costs for future CGT, so there is no immediate tax bill to pay.

Where partners introduce valuable assets into an existing business, for example a property, care should also be taken that this does not trigger unexpected CGT liabilities. In some situations HMRC will argue that amounts being credited to a partner's capital account represents an actual consideration. If the amount credited in this manner exceeds the original cost to the transferor of the asset being introduced, this may well give rise to a CGT liability if the resulting transfer means that other partners have a share in the newly introduced property asset.

Stamp duty land tax (SDLT)

If land and buildings are changing hands then the buyer may have to pay a SDLT charge against the purchase if the amounts involved exceed the current threshold applicable, although there can be some partnership situations in which HMRC does not pursue payment of the SDLT liability. Special advice would need to be taken from an accountant or lawyer with specific tax expertise in this area prior to finalising the transaction.

Inheritance tax (IHT)

Taking in a partner or changing the make-up of a partnership may also have IHT implications. If the change is a commercial arrangement between otherwise unconnected parties then HMRC will normally accept that the arrangements have been entered into for legitimate commercial reasons and that whatever price the shares in the partnership or assets change hands for there is no *gratuitous intent*, in other words this is a commercial deal. As such there is no potential for any IHT liability to arise on any person making a disposal of assets.

If, however, the new individual coming in is a family member or there is some close connection with the existing partner or partners who are handing over a share of their part of the business, then HMRC might invoke market value rules in assessing whether there has been any element of gift by the existing partner or partners.

Where the individuals making such gifts have been in a trading business for more than two years, it is likely that such a gift would qualify in full for 100% Business Property Relief from IHT and as such no liability will arise. However, if this two-year test is not met then the gifts would be regarded as potentially exempt transfers (PETS) and the donor would need to survive seven years for the value of what has been given away to pass out of their estate for IHT purposes.

Value added tax (VAT)

Taking in a new partner will also mean that any existing VAT registration will need to be altered to reflect the new make up of the business partnership and to secure the continuation of the VAT registration number. This is not normally a difficult procedure and involves the submission of some simple forms to HMRC.

Whenever a partner is taken into a business, HMRC should be informed straightaway so that the rules set out earlier about notification are complied with and no penalties for failing to notify HMRC of the existence of a new business to income tax or VAT are inadvertently incurred.

Taxes to consider when starting a partnership

1. Income tax

2. Capital gains tax (CGT)

3. Stamp duty land tax (SDLT)

4. Inheritance tax (IHT)

5. Value added tax (VAT)

Incorporation of a business

Transferring from an income tax business to a limited company liable to CT is a major step and often occurs as a small business grows. The manner in which you choose to incorporate your business can determine the flexibility you have in running it thereafter and may also bring some tax planning opportunities.

It bears repeating that when a limited company is formed it is a legally separate entity from the individual(s) who form the company and it will have its own tax affairs. This is of crucial importance. Many of the compliance failures occur when the owner-manager/shareholder does not properly grasp this essential legal separation.

Transferring an existing business from an unincorporated sole tradership or partnership to a limited company vehicle is different from starting up a business activity inside a limited company from scratch. Although in most cases the incorporation of an existing business can be accomplished without any significant tax liabilities arising, it is very important to recognise that the

"The manner in which you choose to incorporate your business can determine the flexibility you have in running it thereafter and may also bring some tax planning opportunities. "

transfer will be taking place between *connected persons* for tax purposes, i.e. you and the company, and as such there is always the potential for tax liabilities to be incurred.

When you form your own company you will almost certainly be the major shareholder. In many cases you will be the only shareholder, although you may decide to spread the shareholdings around your family to assist with tax planning (as discussed in Chapter 1). Because you control the company by your shareholding you are connected with the company for tax purposes. Thus in principle any transfers of valuable assets between yourself and the company are initially treated as taking place at their market values for tax purposes.

All the taxes must be carefully considered when transferring an existing business to a limited company.

Income tax

The incorporation of an existing business is treated as a cessation of the existing income tax business and this may trigger unexpected and undesirable tax liabilities. It might also accelerate existing and already established income tax liabilities, such as those on the profits of the last tax year. Furthermore, there may have to be adjustments to the capital allowances calculations for the income tax business which can in some situations produce unexpected tax charges.

In most cases these liabilities can be overcome but this will need careful planning and attention from tax advisers. Any transfers of valuable stocks or work-in-progress carried in the balance sheet of the income tax business will take place at market value for income tax purposes unless specific elections are made to transfer them at a lower cost figure. Again this will need careful consideration, but in some cases this may actually help reduce final tax bills for the income tax business. Setting the price that the limited company actually pays for the carried stocks and/or work-in-progress (within limits proscribed by statute) can be a neat and tidy way of transferring these items and may also reduce the cessation income tax liabilities of the sole tradership or partnership.

If there are any unused trading losses in the income tax business it will be essential to ensure that these are used up before the incorporation as far as possible, as the ability to use these once the business has been transferred to the limited company is quite restricted. Basically, they can be used against dividends extracted from the company by the proprietor, but this may not always be possible or practical for quite some time after the incorporation for a variety of reasons. It is better to seek to use these losses up before your existing income tax business ceases if at all possible.

On the positive side, there is a possibility that incorporation may trigger entitlement to any so far unused overlap relief (as discussed earlier) and so may actually lead to a reduction in current year income tax liabilities. This, coupled with the fact that the first CT bill will probably not be due until nine months after the business' first 12-month CTAP comes to an end, could actually produce something of a short *holiday* from tax for the business.

It may also be possible to arrange for the plant and machinery on which you are claiming capital allowances to go across to the new company at prices which facilitate helpful balancing adjustments for income tax purposes, thus reducing income tax liabilities further.

Capital gains tax (CGT)

It is with CGT that the largest potential for problems can occur for an incorporation. Where valuable assets such as property or goodwill are held in an income tax business there is the potential for CGT liabilities to crystallise if these assets are transferred to a limited company.

In most cases this potential liability can be avoided or deferred by choosing one of two specific methods of incorporating the business; through an *exchange for shares* or via a more direct and arguably simpler *gift* method. Both routes have their advantages and disadvantages and both have the potential to trigger tax liabilities.

The gift route has been more popular in recent years as it tends to result in lower overall SDLT liabilities and also may facilitate the retention of some valuable assets in the private hands of the shareholder. The *exchange for shares* route has become less popular recently as it generally involves higher stamp duties.

The incorporation route chosen here will depend upon the particular circumstances of your business and whether or not you wish to retain some assets in your own hands. Choose the method of incorporation carefully and only with specific tax advice from an experienced practitioner in this field.

The two alternative methods of incorporation for CGT purposes can mean that future asset disposals suffer lower CGT liabilities depending upon which route you have chosen.

An incorporation *in exchange for shares* can mean that subsequent asset sales from the company suffer very little tax (although the proceeds are now inside the company).

Taking the *gift* route to incorporation will normally mean much lower capital gains costs for the assets inside the company. However, by using this method some assets can be retained privately outside the company. Furthermore, a directors' loan account balance can sometimes be created with the transferred historic costs of assets such as goodwill being credited inside the company accounts. This loan account balance can then be drawn out by the proprietor, effectively free of tax over the succeeding years.

Consideration should be given to whether assets are retained privately or passed on to the company. Retaining assets privately may mean that on any eventual sale there is only one CGT charge rather than two. If the assets are inside the company and have to be sold, the net of tax proceeds may be later extracted from the company and would then be subjected to tax again at that stage. On the other hand, having assets owned outside a company may mean that access to valuable CGT reliefs, such as entrepreneurs' relief, is not as easily retained for the individual property owner.

Inheritance tax (IHT)

There is usually no question of any IHT liability arising on incorporation of a business because no gratuitous intent is involved. The proprietor of the income tax business transfers the existing business and its assets and liabilities over to his company and normally exchanges direct ownership of his assets for indirect ownership of those same assets via the ownership of shares to the same value. As such there has been no *loss to the donor* – no reduction in the value of this individual's overall wealth – and no IHT liability should arise.

Value added tax (VAT)

Normally when an existing business is transferred to a limited company as a going concern it should be possible to retain the same VAT registration and to have the VAT treatment continue as before with no adjustments being necessary. This is an area to consult with tax advisers about before proceeding.

Summary

There are several key features of any business start-up which must be given close attention from the tax perspective:

- *Type of taxes due* – businesses pay a number of different taxes and it is important to ascertain precisely which liabilities the business will be exposed to and why.

- *Timing* – it will be important to identify when the first and subsequent tax bills are going to arise.

- *Computation* – it will be essential to know what the basis of the calculation of the businesses taxable profits will be and how this is to be accomplished.

- *Planning* – always factor your business tax liabilities into the business plan. Failing to do this leads to severe cash flow problems and in extreme cases can mean business failure.

- *Accounting periods and taxable periods* – different accounting dates can result in liabilities falling due at different times so judicious choices can affect the timing of your businesses tax liabilities significantly.

- *Business changes* – when a business moves through different stages, i.e. partnership or company formation, this can bring tax issues to the fore but may also bring tax planning opportunities as well.

- *Partnership changes* – tax liabilities may be affected as new partners are introduced to a partnership or when they leave. Tax basis periods will be different for existing partners and new partners.

- *Consider all taxes* – do not forget the more peripheral tax liabilities and other charges such as NIC. Although relatively small, overlooking these can lead to significant debts building up over time.

- *Business structure* – this was covered in Chapter 1 but as it is so important it is worth reiterating that the choice of business structure can affect the amount and timing of business tax liabilities very significantly.

4. Compliance and Dealing with the Tax Authorities

Making the right impression

When starting your own business an integral part of the tax planning process is the paperwork necessary to register the business with the official bodies and organisations. Treat this as just part of the business set-up process in the same way as reaching customers, visiting the bank manager or establishing lines of credit with suppliers – it is a fundamental part of good business organisation.

A business that treats its obligations to the tax authorities as important from the outset, and gets them done on time and in an efficient manner, will make a good impression. This is important as it can play a part in the *risk assessment* that your business is given by HMRC. This may well reduce the level of interventions that HMRC will decide to make in the future.

HMRC has inspection rights to your business premises, records and assets which, whilst not necessarily a major concern for a well-run business, can be intrusive and time consuming. The lower their risk assessment and perception of your business as a *problem customer* the less likely HMRC will deem it necessary to investigate.

The main tax obligations of a business

Whenever your business makes profits, sells goods or services, employs people, uses subcontractors, buys and sells property, or is involved in a variety of other transactions, it almost invariably incurs a tax liability of one form or another.

> **"** HMRC has inspection rights to your business premises, records and assets which, whilst not necessarily a major concern for a well-run business, can be intrusive and time consuming. **"**

Taxes are either direct – charged on profits – or indirect – charged on supplies bought and purchases made.

Income tax

A sole trader and each partner in a partnership will have to pay income tax on the profits of their business calculated according to Generally Accepted Commercial Accounting Principles (GAAP). This normally means that you will need an accountant to do your annual financial accounts, although currently this is not a legal obligation in the UK.

Corporation tax

A limited company pays CT on its profits and capital gains, and similarly these must be computed according to GAAP principles. The accounting requirements are more onerous for a limited company and effectively this means that you are obliged to use a qualified accountant to prepare your accounts.

PAYE

As discussed above, the business must deduct a variety of taxes and other charges from employees' salaries and wages, and pay these to HMRC on a monthly basis.

National Insurance (NI)

If your business is a sole tradership or a partnership you will need to register personally for the monthly payment of class 2 NICs.

You will also pay class 4 NICs annually on your income tax self-assessment. Each partner in a partnership business will have to do this.

If you employ people your business must deduct primary class 1 NICs from employees' wages and pay these to HMRC monthly along with employers secondary class 1 NICs.

Value added tax (VAT)

A business whose turnover exceeds the annual thresholds must charge VAT on its taxable supplies and pay VAT on any taxable purchases it makes. The difference between the VAT on these outputs and inputs must be paid to HMRC quarterly along with various other VAT charges, for example charges in respect of business vehicles used privately.

Capital gains tax (CGT)

Capital gains tax is a charge on asset disposals and sometimes on gifts as well. Companies pay CT on their chargeable gains while individuals and partners pay CGT on their chargeable gains. A partnership is not of itself liable to CGT, but instead the partners are regarded as each owning an underlying share of the assets and thus they each pay capital gains individually when an asset in which they share ownership is sold or otherwise disposed of at a taxable gain.

Inheritance tax

Individuals may incur a liability to IHT when they die or make certain gifts during their lifetime. The tax is a charge on the excess of total wealth over the lifetime allowance per individual (currently £325,000). Spouses can effectively bequeath their unused allowance to their surviving spouse.

Broadly, gifts from one individual to another are not taxable if the donor survives seven years from the date of the gift. The tax is charged on the *loss to the donor principle*, which is on the difference between the value of the individuals total estate before the disposal and immediately afterwards. This may not always be the same as the value of the actual gift.

When an individual dies the value of their business is initially included in the total valuation of their estate for IHT purposes. However, in most cases business assets and shares in partnerships or trading companies do not affect an individual's overall IHT liability because currently the UK tax regime provides a 100% relief from IHT on these assets via a scheme known as Business Property Relief. Some assets attract full relief and some attract 50% or nil relief, depending upon their tax status at the time of the individual's death or at the date of a gift. Taking steps to ensure that the valuable assets you have in your business qualify for this relief is of considerable importance. This is discussed in more detail later in the book.

Companies do not normally pay IHT but in some situations close companies can be charged IHT where HMRC takes the view that assets have been transferred by the company. This is extremely rare but in these situations the deemed transfer of value is apportioned among the shareholders and taxed on an attribution basis as if they had made the transfer of value themselves. This is a situation to be avoided if at all possible!

Stamp taxes

There are two main stamp taxes in force in the UK at the moment:

1. *Stamp duty* is broadly payable on transfers of shares in companies and is normally charged at 0.5%.

2. *Stamp duty land tax* is normally payable on purchases of interests in land or leases of land and buildings, and is charged on a sliding scale starting at 0.5% and rising to 4% for values

above £500,000 (with special provisions due to come in after April 2011 for houses costing more than £1m). There are special concessions for some low value residential properties.

Levies and duties

Your business will also have to pay a whole range of other taxes in the course of carrying on its business. These range from insurance premium tax to duty on petrol or diesel fuels, to passenger duties on flights and a range of purchase taxes and levies. In addition there will be business rates payable for the occupation of properties, vehicle excise duties and there may be other regulatory charges for certain businesses – for example data protection and money laundering registration fees for businesses operating in the financial services sector.

Documentation and paperwork

Form filling cannot be avoided at the start-up stage, especially where taxation is concerned. The good thing is that nowadays a business can fulfil most of its start-up tax notifications via the HMRC website. HMRC has some useful content on their website that will provide you with guidance at this stage. For instance, they have useful information on registering a business: **www.hmrc.gov.uk/ct/getting-started/new-company/start-up.htm** and on working for yourself: **www.hmrc.gov.uk/startingup/working-yourself.pdf**

Now let's look at some of the forms that will need to be completed.

Form CWF1 – individuals and partnerships

A newly self-employed sole trader or a new partnership business will have to notify the HMRC of the commencement of the business for income tax and NIC purposes using form CWF1.

If the business is a partnership then each partner will also need to fill this form in to ensure that each is registered as self-employed for income tax. This form must be completed even if the individual already completes an annual self-assessment.

VAT 1 – all liable businesses

If the business is going to exceed the VAT registration turnover thresholds then it will need to register straightaway for VAT using the online registration system (found at **www.hmrc.gov.uk/vat/start/register**).

CT forms – companies

If your business is going to be run via a limited company then it will need to register for CT using form CT41G (found at **www.hmrc.gov.uk/ctsa**).

Companies are usually formed using a company formation agent, accountant or solicitor and must be registered with Companies

House in the UK for the submission of their annual accounts. Note that Limited Liability Partnerships also have to do this but ordinary partnerships do not.

Detailed instructions from HMRC about starting a company and the obligations for CT can be found on their website (**www.hmrc.gov.uk/ct/getting-started/new-company**).

Employees – setting up a PAYE scheme

If your business is taking on employees it will also need to set up a PAYE scheme so that you can deduct tax and NIC from them and deal with the other employers' obligations, such as sick pay and maternity pay, that you will be obliged to undertake on behalf of HMRC.

A new employer can register online to obtain all the necessary forms and paperwork together with a detailed starter pack to assist in this process:

www.hmrc.gov.uk/paye/intro

You should always keep full copies of the documentation sent to HMRC, whether in hard copy or electronic format, as evidence that the business has met and fulfilled its obligations.

Time limits and telling the tax authorities

Getting the various tax notification forms completed and submitted to the tax authorities is a legal obligation and has to be done within certain time limits. If these time limits are not met there will be financial penalties imposed on the business by HMRC and these can be costly. Missing deadlines will also earn the business an adverse *risk rating* as the result of a poor compliance track record.

Income tax

The commencement of a new source of income has to be notified to the HMRC within six months of the end of the tax year in which the business starts.

There is a penalty for not meeting this notification obligation, which is based on the amount of net tax due but unpaid at 31 January in the tax year following the one in which the liability first arises. Thus where you fail to notify chargeability by 5 October, there will normally be no penalty payable if all your tax is paid in full by the following 31 January.

National Insurance notification

A self-employed sole trader or partners in a newly established partnership must register for class 2 NICs within three months of the end of the calendar month in which the business started to trade.

The penalty for failure to meet this notification deadline is currently £100 per individual or business partner.

Corporation tax

Any company which is liable to CT for an accounting period must notify HMRC of this within 12 months of the end of that accounting period, unless it has already received a notice requiring the company to submit a CT return.

Also, a company must notify HMRC when it first comes within the charge to CT or comes back into charge after a period of dormancy, no later than three months after the accounting period begins.

For companies failing to notify CT within the appropriate time limits the penalty can be up to 100% of the unpaid CT liability for the accounting period in question if it is outstanding 12 months after the end of the accounting period.

VAT

A trader who is liable for VAT based on the last 12 months' turnover must notify HMRC and register for VAT within 30 days of the end of the relevant month.

A trader who is liable for registration on an estimate of turnover in the next 30 days must notify and register for VAT within 30 days of the end of the relevant month.

The penalties for failing to notify are tax geared and are a percentage of the VAT depending upon the length of the period involved, ranging from 5% for periods below nine months and up to 15% for periods over 18 months.

Special tax schemes

Some businesses can use special tax regimes if they meet certain criteria. HMRC offers a variety of schemes that may provide simplifications or relaxations of the tax system in particular circumstances and could make running your business easier or more straightforward.

It is worthwhile taking a look at the available schemes when you start up to make sure that you are not missing out. Some of these schemes can mean a saving and some have a cash flow benefit.

Modified PAYE schemes for expatriates

If you have employees who frequently travel overseas or your business involves bringing in workers from overseas on a regular basis then you should contact your tax office and ask for information on modified PAYE. These special schemes can considerably simplify the complex tax administration which can arise when dealing with visitors from overseas, or for your employees working overseas, especially in countries where the terms of specific double tax treaties may apply.

This is an area of tax compliance which is fraught with traps for the unwary and some awkward computation issues can arise, which can result in undesirable cash flow consequences for your business if not dealt with well in advance.

HMRC offers three schemes:

1. The short-term visitor scheme, under which relaxations of the normal PAYE obligations can be permitted.

2. Net of tax credit relief (where you might otherwise have to pay PAYE both at home and overseas for your employees).

3. Tax equalisation PAYE (for foreign national workers coming to the UK to work).

All of these are relatively straightforward to put into operation and can save your business a mass of otherwise complex and time consuming administration. They can only be put in place, however, with the agreement of your PAYE tax office so contact them to get this set up.

Simplified PAYE schemes

Where you have a very small number of employees HMRC can also authorise the operation of what is known as simplified PAYE and again this will save you a lot of time and compliance costs so is well worth investigating.

VAT cash accounting

VAT is normally payable by reference to the businesses' sales invoices issued and expenses incurred – following the accruals and prepayments basis used in normal commercial accounting. However, this can mean that you have to pay VAT to HMRC on the basis of issued but unpaid invoices.

Under the VAT cash accounting scheme, VAT is accounted for to HMRC using the actual payments and receipts of the business during the VAT reporting period, usually quarterly. This means that a business gets automatic bad debt relief on any sales invoices that don't get paid and does not have to pay VAT to HMRC that it has not yet received from its customers.

Other VAT schemes

Other special schemes that are available for VAT registered traders are:

- *Flat rate VAT accounting* – this involves operating a much simplified method of computing VAT output tax on your sales. It is done by calculating your VAT payments as a percentage of your total VAT-inclusve turnover. VAT need not be calculated for each individual invoice, but just for the total of VAT-inclusive sales proceeds.

- *Annual accounting* – although not suitable for everyone this can mean that a business, subject to meeting certain criteria, need only complete one VAT return annually.

Dispensations and PAYE agreements

A business will often have specific obligations to make returns to HMRC in respect of a whole range of expenses and benefits that it pays or makes available to its employees. In many cases the HRMC gets no extra tax as a result of these returns because very often the employee can make a matching expense claim on their own income tax self-assessment return against the reported benefits or expenses.

HMRC will permit an employer to opt out of making the annual returns of expenses and benefits (form P11D) if the employer can persuade them that the income of the employees is matched by an equivalent expenses claim each year. The department will then grant a formal dispensation, which will probably be reviewed thereafter once every five or six years. This can save your business an awful lot of paperwork, although you and your employees must still keep records of expenses and benefits.

Similarly, where there are taxable benefits for employees an employer can offer to make a one-off annual payment to HMRC to settle the tax and NICs arising on a grossed up basis rather than having to report the benefits return form and then leaving the employees to pay the tax. This is called a *PAYE Settlement Agreement*.

Business payroll obligations

Setting up and running a payroll and operating PAYE and NICs on your employees' earnings is probably one of the most onerous tax compliance tasks that any business has to undertake.

Decide who is an employee

The first task is to decide who is an employee, which might not be as easy as it sounds! It is common for businesses to treat someone who works for them or on their behalf as self-employed or as a freelance subcontractor or consultant. This is a dangerous thing to do and should not be entered into lightly.

Many individuals insist that they are self-employed when they are not. Employment status is not a matter of personal preference but is baed on the facts of the relationship between worker and work provider. Treating someone who is in fact an employee as self-employed means you risk running up a sizeable tax and NIC bill, plus possibly interest and penalties.

Whether or not someone actually is self-employed requires a review of a considerable number of factors relating to their working relationship with you and your business. This is a controversial area of tax law and the risks of getting this wrong are high. Wherever there is any doubt about a worker's tax status the sensible options are to treat

> **"** Employment status is not a matter of personal preference but is based on the facts of the relationship between worker and work provider. **"**

them as an employee or to seek specialist advice. In specific cases it will be necessary to ensure that properly drafted contracts of engagement are put in place which accurately reflect the day-to-day facts of the working relationship between you and the individual.

The PAYE regulations impose an absolute obligation on a business to deduct tax and NICs from employees' earnings and to account for this to HMRC. HMRC takes the employment status of workers very seriously and has specialist status compliance officers who review the situation of employees during inspection visits.

The HMRC will first seek to recover any underpayments from the employer, not initially from the employee. In order to avoid this recovery an employer needs to be able to demonstrate that they have at worst *made a simple error in good faith having taken all reasonable care.* This means that whenever you take someone on to work for you and you decide that they are self-employed then at the very least you have to be able to show that you have actively considered and carefully reviewed their tax status, and made a reasoned and carefully argued decision based on a thorough review of all the facts.

Operate PAYE

Once you have decided that someone is actually an employee you must put them on the payroll as a new starter and deduct tax and NICs from their wages/salary and any other monetary remuneration. There are a host of rules here and HMRC will provide a set-up and starter pack as soon as you register a new PAYE scheme with them.

All employees will be taxed under PAYE according to a tax code issued by HMRC. This will be on form P45 that the new employee gives you from their last job. If they do not have a P45 you *must* fill out and ask them to sign a P46 which tells the employer what particular tax code to operate for a short period, pending issue of a formal code from HMRC.

Employees are also liable to income tax on certain expenses and benefits with which you provide them in the course of their employment. Your business has to make an annual return of these expenses and benefits to HMRC by 6 July after the end of each tax year on form P11D, unless you have obtained a dispensation from HMRC as described earlier.

Expenses and benefits that are returned on form P11D are also liable to class 1A NICs. This is payable at the same rates as class 1 NICs on employees earnings (currently 12.8%) and has to be paid to HMRC in July each year.

Other statutory schemes under the PAYE system

An employer also has a legal obligation to operate certain non-tax systems on behalf of the government. These are:

- statutory sick pay

- statutory maternity and paternity pay

- adoption pay

- student loans deduction scheme

All of these require an employer to account to the HMRC for certain payments to your employees or to make deductions from their earnings. Most of them are fairly simple to operate and take only a little time individually, but they all add to the administrative burden.

A business is also responsible for making tax deductions under the Construction Industry Subcontractors (CIS) deduction scheme if it operates in the construction industry or, if it does not, in certain specified circumstances when the business carries on defined construction operations in the course of its activities. This entails making tax deductions from subcontractors who are not entitled to receive their income gross (according to their registration status with the tax authorities) and paying those sums to HMRC along with monthly PAYE tax and NIC deductions.

A business must also provide employees with information about non-tax schemes such as the stakeholder pension scheme.

A business may also be responsible for making deductions from an employee's earnings if the courts issue an "Attachment of Earnings Order". This normally happens when an employee has been the subject of a court order, for example for non-payment of child support or similar statutory obligations.

Fundamentally, of course, a business must pay its employees the right amount of salary or wages. This means ensuring that you comply at the very least with the national minimum wage regulations. Failure to do so can lead to fines and prosecution.

Summary

Tax obligations must be factored in as an integral part of the business planning and setting-up process.

The key issues are:

- What taxes will be payable on profits/income?

- When will those taxes fall due?

- How soon must the HMRC be told of the business start-up?

- What special regimes and options can be used to help plan tax liabilities?

The key actions to be taken will be:

- Complete the correct notification forms and paperwork.

- Put in place control systems to ensure that the notifications are in place on time.

- Start planning early to meet the relevant tax deadlines.

- Ensure that the business makes proper provisions from its profits to pay its taxes.

- Write tax compliance into the business plan from the outset.

5. HMRC Tax Investigations – Compliance Checks

Introduction

A tax investigation by HMRC can be stressful and expensive for a business. HMRC has the right to enquire into all tax returns and it also has the right to carry out compliance checks on tax affairs and other aspects of a business even when a return has not recently been submitted. The tax laws now in force give HMRC very significant powers of inspection and review, and the ability to ask detailed questions about tax returns, tax calculations and other documents used for the purposes of taxation.

It is important to understand that a business must cooperate fully with the HMRC when they ask questions about tax affairs. Apart from *relevance* and *reasonableness* there are

> **"** HMRC has the right to enquire into all tax returns and it also has the right to carry out compliance checks on tax affairs and other aspects of a business even when a return has not recently been submitted. **"**

very few practical restrictions on the information a tax inspector can request from you about your tax affairs and those of your business. The *relevance* restriction means that where the inspector can show that a request for a specific piece of information will enable HMRC to better understand how the business works, how its accounts reflect the transaction recorded in its business records, the sorts of activities it carries on, what services it offers to its customers or what types of good it sells, then the inspector is probably entitled to that information.

Where a business submits a tax return the inspector is entitled to check that the return and its financial accounts produce a reasonable and fair measure of the business profitability, so it is *reasonable* for him to be able to seek access to and review the business' financial records and other supplementary financial information in the business' possession in order to carry out that checking procedure. On the other hand the size and scale of a business' activities may preclude the inspector from carrying out very detailed checking into every aspect and may mean that he has to restrict his reviews to sampling and specific areas of information.

Whilst there is no statutory limit on the amount of detail an inspector can ask for, it would probably be regarded as unreasonable for him to seek to see every single record where those records are very extensive and contain a mass of detail that may not actually help the inspector understand the business' financial affairs better or enable him to form a reasonable view of the accuracy of the business' self-assessment tax returns.

You should certainly ensure that your tax adviser represents your interests properly and robustly and keeps a check on what the inspector asks for during the progress of the enquiry. In most cases it is important to recognise that this is a normal statutory process and the inspector is normally well within his rights to ask questions about your tax affairs as well as those of your business.

Why a business may be selected for investigation

What is a tax compliance check?

HMRC carries out compliance checks into business' tax affairs for a variety of reasons and in a number of ways. Such enquiries can range from a specific question about a technical aspect of a business' financial accounts or tax calculations, through to a more detailed review of all the technical aspects of the tax returns, to a full in-depth review of the totality of the tax affairs of the business and its proprietors.

Clearly the type of enquiries – or *compliance checks* – will vary enormously with the size and complexity of the business. In some cases only one specific aspect of a return or a set of financial accounts will be reviewed. In other cases the review may encompass several such points. Others will require detailed access to business records and may extend to meetings with the business owners or managers so as to enable the tax officials to get a better understanding of the business and how it operates.

How to avoid HMRC compliance checks

- Aim for a low risk rating

- Demonstrate good control systems

- Avoid record-keeping failures

- Avoid simple tax offences

- Communicate with HMRC properly (by providing the right information) and on-time

---

Why enquiries happen

There are a multitude of reasons why a particular business may be chosen for review by HMRC. Selection does not automatically mean that HMRC is assuming that something is wrong. The UK's self-assessed tax system for business means that HMRC is given an absolute right to ask questions about any tax return as a corollary to the system that requires taxpayers to tell the HMRC what their own tax liability is.

Tax returns are filed under self-assessment by taxpayers who compute their own liability as part of that process. HMRC is not involved in the calculation process at the submission stage and simply accepts the tax returns subject to some basic verification steps. Where HMRC decides to check a tax return or start a compliance check it does not mean it is challenging a return's accuracy at that stage, it is merely exercising its statutory right to review the entries made in the accounts.

If, however, the inspector does find that something is wrong – perhaps where an inadvertent mistake has occurred – he has the right to satisfy himself that there are no other errors elsewhere in the return and so a more thorough check may commence.

Profiling and risk assessment

Information gathering

HMRC has access to a great variety of information about all taxpayers. It carries out a intelligence gathering across a range of information sources which includes all other government departments and agencies, and the examination of publicly available information. The types of sources HMRC may use include local press and publications, cross references from other taxpayers' files and a host of information which may flow through to the taxpayer's record from research. All this information will be reviewed and form part of the overall risk rating which may be allocated to a particular case reference. The higher the risk rating the higher the chances of being selected for detailed review. The department's intelligence gathering units will collate this information and disseminate it internally.

Aim for a low risk rating

Businesses are allocated risk scores by the HMRC as part of its process for selecting compliance checks. Risk weightings are based on the type of business, the taxpayer's tax track record, whether there have been problems in the past and specific compliance failures, for example the previous imposition of interest and penalty charges. The higher the risk rating the more likely it is that a particular business may be included within the pool pre-selected for review or for possible enquiry at a future date.

A business' objective, then, should be to seek to have a low risk rating. This will be achieved in the first instance by having a good tax compliance record. This means getting the basics right; such as getting tax returns in on time and paying taxes – including VAT, income tax or CT, PAYE and other liabilities – on time so that the business does not incur penalties and interest charges.

Demonstrate good control systems

When an inspection visit takes place (for example routine PAYE inspection compliance checks may be carried out by HMRC on your business payroll records) it is important to show that your business is organised, efficient and well controlled. Giving the right impression and demonstrating that such matters are dealt with properly and in a timely fashion with no compliance errors will again result in a lower overall risk score on your taxpayer record and hence reduce the likelihood of detailed enquiries being carried out later.

This is not about hiding anything from HMRC – it is about showing your business to the department as one that is well run and keeping its tax affairs in order and up-to-date.

All taxpayer records are accorded a core risk rating; either low, medium or high. It is likely that HMRC will regard some business sectors and types of business as potentially of higher risk than others. Taxpayers with especially complex tax affairs or extensive business and personal financial interests can inevitably expect to be allocated a higher risk rating than a small sole trader business running a low turnover.

In practice the affairs of a small business are unlikely to be reviewed in detail as frequently as those of larger, more complex businesses. Experience has proved to the HMRC that these smaller cases rarely produce results which justify the effort put into reviewing them. On the other hand all taxpayer records must be within the scope of the compliance checks regime to ensure fairness and coverage across the board, and also to provide the deterrent element that the possibility of any business being chosen brings.

Have a good record-keeping system

A large number of tax compliance checks and compliance failures arise simply because a business either did not put in place a good record keeping-system at the start or failed subsequently to keep its records up to date. When a business starts up HMRC offers business support services, one of which is checking the sort of records that you are keeping. Showing HMRC officers that records of business transactions are well kept, comprehensive and reliable will demonstrate that the risk of error is low and that your tax compliance is likely deserving of a lower overall risk rating.

When a business keeps poor records of its income and expenditures it becomes almost inevitable that compliance failures will occur. In this situation the accountant or auditor that identifies such a failure will inevitably have to make an appropriate adjustment and may also have to report the error to HRMC as part of their compliance obligations when dealing with your tax affairs.

You should also recognise that when a serious tax compliance failure has been identified by your accountant or tax adviser (this may include simple negligence), it will probably have to be the subject of a report to the Serious Organised Crime Agency due to obligations accountants face under the Money Laundering Regulations and the Proceeds of Crime Act 2002. They have no choice about doing this and will not inform you that they have done so. Furthermore, there is no minimum reporting limit so even simple compliance failures may be reported in this way and may subsequently lead to HMRC starting a review of your business' tax affairs.

Build up a good track record

A business with a record of poor compliance and failures in compliance such as late submission of tax returns and accounts, and late payment of taxes, is inevitably likely to be regarded by HMRC as more deserving of its compliance checks attention. If a business cannot get its simple compliance obligations right and completed on time then it is perhaps understandable that the department will view it as more likely to be committing other tax offences or failing its record-keeping obligations. Keeping up to date and paying your taxes on time will not mean that you can actually prevent a tax compliance check taking place, because there are a whole host of reasons why such reviews can begin, but it is an important starting point.

Be alert to information received

When a business is selected as a possibility for enquiry, the official dealing with the case will pull together a risk analysis pack containing all available data he can find. This will entail him using all research tools and online data sources at his disposal.

The HMRC receives a lot of data from informants. Whilst this may not seem appropriate to some, it is a well-established part of the flow of information to the department. Indeed in some instances the department will even pay for information. A lot of the information disclosed to HMRC from such sources is anonymous and non-attributable and as such is not actually usable as evidence in a formal sense. However, it can create a negative first impression of a business.

It is also worth mentioning that some of this anonymous tip-off information is malicious and inaccurate. Inspectors are well aware of this and will rarely give it much credence. Businesses that involve some element of nuisance to their neighbours are often victim to this sort of treatment and you should be aware of the potential for this to happen. Former employees and ex-spouses are also one of the common sources of vindictive information flowing to the HMRC in this manner.

Use tax schemes with care

Where an individual has utilised structured tax planning devices in the past, this might be regarded by HMRC as a reason for subjecting an individual taxpayer's record to more detailed scrutiny. The willingness of a tax expert to get involved in structured tax avoidance devices has been regarded in recent years as perhaps indicative of a more adventurous attitude to tax compliance, and hence can be expected to be used as a possible reason for regarding a taxpaying client as deserving of a higher risk rating than that allocated to other taxpayers.

This should always be borne in mind when you consider whether to use these sorts of tax planning techniques. This is not to say that such techniques do not have a part to play in your overall tax planning strategy – I discuss some of them in more detail later – but you should be aware of the likely impact their use might have on the HMRC's overall view of your tax affairs.

Complex taxpayers receive more attention

The affairs of wealthy taxpayers are accorded special attention by HMRC. It has specialist departments and officers devoted to dealing with High Net Worth Individuals and their businesses. If your personal tax affairs are complex, or if you have a range of business and personal financial interests and as such need specialist help and support from the HMRC, then you can expect that this will result in your personal risk rating being somewhat higher than those with simpler affairs.

This is not always a cause for concern because it can mean that your affairs are dealt with at a higher and more experienced level within the department. It does mean, however, that the prospect of you being the subject of more detailed and regular compliance checks, and personal tax reviews, are higher than average.

Be aware of sector-specific risks

Some business sectors and activities have traditionally been viewed by HMRC as more likely to be guilty of compliance failures. Businesses employing large numbers of casual workers or seasonal workforces, or with a history of cash income or payments, inevitably attract attention. These businesses should pay extra attention to PAYE and general tax compliance by such businesses.

Take advice on technical accounting issues

Company accounts are likely to be reviewed in some detail where they exhibit more complex accounting and technical issues. HMRC now employs its own qualified accounting personnel to review more complex areas of tax and accounting such as transfer pricing, inter-company management charges, stock and work in progress valuation, loan arrangements, large purchase financing, factoring arrangements, and deductible provisions and reserves, and a whole range of other technical areas where there may be disputes about the correct accounting and tax treatment.

If your business has unusual or complex accounting issues or applies specific or unusual accounting treatments to expenses or receipts, you should ensure that you have taken specialist advice to ensure that these are being dealt with properly.

Be alert to the potential for spin-off

It is inevitable that in reviewing the affairs of one business HMRC officials will come into possession of information about other businesses, perhaps yours, that the other taxpayer deals with. It is important to recognise that cross-fertilisation of information is an important source of enquiries for HMRC. What appears in one business' records should frequently have a corresponding entry in the record of another business and may be used by HMRC as a reason to consider your business worthy of attention.

Avoid simple tax offences

One of the most common reasons that tax compliance checks start is the comparison of information in the HMRC's possession with the taxpayer's tax returns and business accounts. Banks, for example, provide the department on a regular basis with reports of interest paid on bank deposit accounts to individual customers. If someone's tax return does not obviously include the interest on a deposit account that HMRC have been notified about, then this may be queried as a possible omission from a tax return. If interest is omitted from the return, even if it has been taxed at source, this is a tax offence and case law has established that this will give the inspector the right to carry out more detailed enquiries on that individual's tax affairs to establish that there have not been other omissions or more serious tax offences.

It is not that uncommon to see bank interest omitted from a tax return. Small amounts earned on old deposit accounts are easily overlooked, so it is important that you keep good records of your investment accounts and savings products as the HMRC will generally know already what interest or income you have received from such investments. An omission of a small amount of interest is a tax offence and no matter how minor it can be used as justification for a more in-depth review.

Adopt preventative measures

Keep good records

This cannot be stressed enough. Most tax compliance failures arise through simple record-keeping errors or failures. When a tax inspector carries out a review, many of the problems identified arise because the business records fail to provide enough detail or information about specific receipts or expenses, or fail to record them in the correct manner in the accounting system.

Simple record-keeping failures can lead to inaccurate reporting of business profits in a variety of ways so ensuring that you have an accurate and comprehensive record-keeping system is essential. Nowadays most businesses operate a computerised system, indeed these are now so cheap to buy and so easy to use that HMRC almost expects a business to run their record keeping system this way.

Communicate with the tax office

The business that keeps in touch with its tax office and the particular departments that it interacts with on a regular basis, for example the PAYE section, and establishes good lines of communication will find that it tends to receive more proactive treatment. A good relationship with the tax officials you deal with regularly is essential.

Larger businesses, especially companies, will have their own customer relations manager appointed to look after their affairs. Keeping in touch and establishing regular communication either directly or through your own tax advisers will go a long way to enabling any problems to be dealt with expeditiously.

Pay attention to risk assessment

A business should be aware of the process of risk assessment and therefore do all that it can to seek to ensure that it has a low risk rating, or one that is as low as reasonably practical in the context of the business sector within which it operates.

Summary

The following represents a brief summary of important do's and don'ts which should help anyone facing a tax enquiry or compliance check of any kind to deal with it effectively:

- *Don't panic.* Most tax compliance checks are settled quite quickly and painlessly, and are resolved by simple reference to your business or personal financial records.

- *Don't delay.* Providing timely and accurate responses to HMRC queries generally means that the review is less traumatic and resolved speedily.

- *Do cooperate.* Providing quick and comprehensive answers to inspectors' questions gives the right impression and can mean a business receives favourable treatment with penalties, if errors do come to light.

- *Do provide evidence.* Backup all statements and explanations with reference to documentary evidence and financial records. Explanations are fine but specific documentary evidence is much more persuasive.

- *Do seek advice.* It is rare that an unrepresented taxpayer copes as well during the course of a compliance check as someone who has professional representation – seek assistance from an accountant or chartered tax adviser.

- *Don't guess.* It is very common, especially where a review covers earlier years, for you not to be able remember or recall exactly what went on. Never provide estimates about information from earlier years – always refer back to records, even if this requires extensive research.

- *Do test all the inspector's assumptions and computations.* Tax reviews often involve comparative calculations being produced by the tax official with which to test the business records and returns. This almost inevitably involves some element of estimation and the making of certain assumptions. These should always be tested exhaustively as it is often in the detail of these calculations that the reasons for apparent discrepancies and differences are to be found and challenged. Take time to examine and test inspectors' assertions in great detail.

- *Do provide accurate information at interviews.* Compliance checks often involve face-to-face meetings and interviews. Whilst these are by no means obligatory and no taxpayer can be forced to attend such a meeting, they can be an extremely cost-effective and constructive means of passing on a lot of detailed information in a very short space of time. However, it is important to ensure they are useful and that you provide accurate information. It is easy to give incorrect information in the heat of the moment so ensure that you take your time to deal with these meetings properly. Above all make sure any matters discussed are properly recorded.

- *Do keep the case moving.* If you have provided the inspector with information and records, agree a timescale for the review to take place and hold them to it. Cases can otherwise drag on unnecessarily, which is not in the interest of your business.

- *Don't agree in a hurry.* There is always a temptation to agree to computations and proposed settlement figures during the course of a review. Taking just a little time to check and review proposals often pays dividends in the long run.

- *Do conduct detailed research.* Questions asked in the course of an enquiry will often require detailed examination of historical records. Make sure this is done properly as attention to detail here can be rewarding later.

- *Do prepare fully for meetings.* It is often at enquiry meetings that cases are resolved one way or another and this is a good opportunity to put across crucial information decisively. It is imperative that you prepare thoroughly for any such meetings, and have ready access to briefing notes and important documents. A poorly prepared meeting can lead to a poorly handled review. A well researched and prepared meeting often leads to an early and productive resolution of HMRC's enquiries.

- *Do know who you are dealing with.* If a records inspection is to take place at your business premises find out who is coming and what their particular interest and expertise is. It may be that you will need a particular person in the business or from your accountants or tax advisers present who can deal with specific issues that the HMRC intend to raise.

- *Do be prepared to negotiate.* Most tax compliance checks are settled by some form of compromise when errors or omission come to light, especially where penalties are sought by the HMRC. Take a pragmatic view and be prepared to compromise in order to get the matter resolved.

Part Two

Running A Business

Introduction: The Climate for Tax Planning

A business looking to find legitimate ways of reducing its overall tax burden must take note of the government's attitude to perceived tax avoidance. Governments have shown themselves to be increasingly willing to introduce new legislation to counter perceived abuses of the tax system and to take court action against attempts at tax avoidance. Specific legislation was introduced in 2004 under which structured and marketed tax avoidance schemes have to be formally notified to HMRC by their sponsors or promoters (and in some cases by their users), within specified time limits or financial penalties can be imposed. Since these rules were introduced, a large number of these schemes have been struck out by HMRC using targeted anti-avoidance legislation.

Part Two is concerned with identifying those aspects of the tax affairs of the business person which, if paid the correct and timely attention they deserve, will work to significantly reduce overall tax bills. Many businesses pay more tax and NICs than they need to simply because they do not identify all the different aspects of their financial affairs that combine to make up their complete tax picture.

Tax avoidance and tax evasion

Tax planning means acceptable tax avoidance, not tax evasion. Some people seem to think that identifying exactly where this boundary lies is the holy grail of tax planning. Tax evasion is illegal – it should not be contemplated at all. Anyone attempting tax evasion will almost certainly face prosecution, heavy fines and possibly even a custodial sentence.

Tax avoidance can be defined as *the use of the tax regime in legitimate ways to reduce or eliminate a tax liability*. This is, however, an oversimplification.

A simple example of tax avoidance would be using an Individual Savings Account (ISA) as an investment approach rather than an ordinary savings account. The interest on the former is non-taxable whilst the interest on the latter is. A more complex example of tax avoidance might

> **"** Tax evasion is illegal – it should not be contemplated at all. Any business person attempting tax evasion will almost certainly face prosecution, heavy fines and possibly even a custodial sentence. **""**

be the use by a company of an Employee Benefit Trust to grant loans to its employees rather than bonuses. The loans should suffer a much lower rate of taxation than the equivalent bonuses otherwise would (these loans do not have to be paid back in the same way as a standard loan, meaning the arrangement can work to the advantage of employer and employee).

The difference between these approaches is that an ISA is a government approved, tax favoured savings product specifically designed to encourage saving among the wider population, while the Employee Benefit Trust is a highly structured tax avoidance device that has attracted a lot of attempts to curtail its use by HMRC. Paying loans to employees in this way has been a widely used CT and employment tax avoidance device by larger businesses for some years now and to date the practice continues.

It is likely to be the subject of a detailed review by HMRC and it is possible that new anti-avoidance legislation will be introduced to limit the practice.

What is important from the perspective of this book is that there are legitimate and straightforward ways for a business to reduce its overall tax burden.

Government guidelines

Unfortunately in recent years governments seem to have adopted an attitude which increasingly blurs the boundaries between tax avoidance and tax evasion to the extent that honest taxpayers may have arrived at the belief that even relatively straightforward tax planning is perceived as unacceptable by the authorities. This represents something of a change in the attitude of policymakers to tax planning and tax avoidance which businesses need to bear in mind when considering what strategies to use in their day-to-day tax affairs.

Tax planning and the courts

Since the 1970s the UK courts have increasingly shown themselves wiling to strike down adventurous tax structures where a high degree of artificiality is present in the arrangements involved in putting a plan into action. Numerous tax avoidance strategies have been developed for CT, CGT, IHT and a variety of other liabilities. Some have succeeded and some have not.

An artificial structure might be described as one which involves a series of sequential transactions, some of which have no obvious commercial purpose by themselves and which only become clear when looked at in the context of the overall strategy. An example might be the use of an

> **"** Since the 1970s the UK courts have increasingly shown themselves wiling to strike down adventurous tax structures where a high degree of artificiality is present in the arrangements involved. **"**

Employee Benefit Trust, as described above, to extract profit from a company in a tax deductible form which is then only taxed on the recipient employees as a benefit in kind at a much reduced rate of income tax.

Those schemes that have succeeded have generally been the ones that have a significant degree of commercial underpinning and justification as well as a tax planning motive. Those that have failed have been the highly artificial and structured schemes which lack a fundamental commercial objective.

Schemes were also developed which introduced an element of risk in an attempt to counter the view of the courts that where strategies involved high levels of certainty about the destination of the plans then they were to be viewed as artificial rather than genuine commercial ventures. While this may have been successful in some cases, courts now view the introduction of artificial risk in as equally a negative fashion as they will view circular or linear tax avoidance schemes involving artificial transactions that had no genuine commercial purposes.

Courts have also been willing to counter tax strategies which seek to take advantage of the phraseology or form of specific pieces of legislation, and have developed what has become known as the purposive interpretation of tax law – this means they look beyond the actual wording of legislation to identify not only what it was intended to do but what it was not intended to facilitate.

Thus where schemes have been devised in an attempt to avoid the operation of the detailed PAYE regulations and the charges of NIC on employees' remuneration, the courts have shown themselves willing to strike these strategies down, especially where the legislation was being deliberately interpreted in a manner which might technically look correct but where – in the view of the courts – the strategies were clearly operating outside of the original intention of the specific regulations being interpreted. An example would be a strategy to offer employees interests in life insurance products which could subsequently be surrendered for cash, instead of paying them a straightforward bonus. This would be an attempt to circumvent the NIC and PAYE regulations which would normally apply to such bonuses.

Summary

Life for the tax planner is getting a lot tougher. Anyone seeking to mitigate their tax liabilities needs to bear this in mind when devising ways and means to reduce their overall business tax burden.

Simple strategies can often be the best. A company executive with an expensive company car would be paying a lot of tax on the benefit in kind through his or her PAYE code. By taking the car outside the company and funding it with extra salary (subject to tax and NIC of course), the net effect may well be that the taxable benefit on the car for the employee is eliminated. Whilst the extra salary would still be taxable at the employee's marginal income tax rate, the elimination of the large taxable benefit on the car will often result in an overall reduction in personal tax bills. This is simple tax structuring and it is not tax avoidance.

An alternative approach would be to swap the car for a smaller low emissions vehicle (creating less than 100 grams per kilometre of carbon dioxide emissions) which may reduce tax bills by 20% or more. A more adventurous vehicular tax plan might be to have your company buy a vehicle that technically qualifies as a van and then seek to be taxed on the relatively small benefit in kind that such vehicles commonly attract these days. Of course the definition of what is a van is of itself quite controversial and there is a question over whether this would be a move towards more *structured* – and more controversial – tax planning.

It is clear that it behoves all businesses to pay close attention to the potential savings that they can make by reducing their tax burden as far as possible within the law. A business can save a lot of money in this way, but bear in mind that you may attract the attention of the tax authorities if you pursue tax planning aggressively.

6. Business Tax Bills

Introduction

This chapter identifies the aspects of your business that produce its tax liabilities and suggests areas to which you should pay attention when seeking to mitigate them. It concentrates on how business profits arise and how they are computed.

The type of business you run and the structure within which you operate will affect how and when your tax bills arise. By developing a close understanding of this structure you will inevitably gain a better understanding of how and why your tax bills accrue and what you may be able to do to reduce them.

You should start by gaining a basic understanding of generally accepted commercial accounting principles (GAAP) and ensure that these are being operated correctly.

Next it will be worthwhile looking at the regime for tax expense reliefs and deductions that operates in connection with the financial accounts of commercial businesses and the way these interact with the formal tax computations that will go to HMRC.

Subsequently you should look at how business owners pay tax and how their profits are regarded as taxable on them or their business entity. When someone extracts cash from a business, particularly a limited company, this is normally when tax liabilities arise so it is crucial to look at how, why and when this is done and to consider if you are doing it in the most practical way available to you and your business.

You should also pay close attention to your significant personal expenditure items which will not normally attract tax relief but must be funded out of your own taxed income. Interest on a personal mortgage, school fees, the costs of running a private car, etc., are all expenses that have to be paid out of salary or dividends after tax has been deducted. These do not normally attract tax relief as they are not normally paid through the business but by you personally. However, examining the overall business expenditure structure carefully may indicate opportunities by which matters might be arranged more tax effectively.

Adopt a holistic approach

It is important to reiterate that it is essential always to regard the business and yourself as separate *persons* and also to have a holistic approach to taxation. All tax liabilities and all aspects of your business and personal financial affairs should be regarded as potentially interlinked. One may affect the other.

This is especially the case in a limited company because companies and people are separate bodies by law. With unincorporated businesses this is not strictly the case, but it helps the planning process considerably to keep the two areas of finance – business and personal – rigorously separate. By regarding all businesses as separate entities you will probably gain a better idea of what the effects of business and personal transactions will be on your overall tax position.

Proper accounting practice and timing issues

When you prepare your tax returns each year the most important aspect of this process is the preparation of the business' financial accounts. Tax law requires that accounts and financial statements have to be prepared using GAAP in order to properly reflect the financial results of the business so as to produce the right taxable profits to go on your tax returns. For most people this will mean the use of an accountant to produce accounts and tax statements – this is not a legal obligation for the unincorporated business but it is probably advisable.

> **Tax law requires that accounts and financial statements have to be prepared using GAAP in order to properly reflect the financial results of the business so as to produce the right taxable profits to go on your tax returns.**

Accounting principles follow long established financial reporting standards that qualified accountants have to follow when preparing your financial statements. It is important to recognise that these can have a specific and major impact on when and how the profits of your business were earned and hence when the taxable profits arise.

When expenses are incurred

Certain principles, for example cost recognition under the *prepayments and accruals* concepts, mean that expenses are deemed to arise when they are incurred, which is not necessarily at the same time at which they are paid. Thus, if you incur an expense before the end of your financial accounting period and receive the invoice for that expense then it has been *incurred* for the purposes of those accounts and must be reflected therein as a closing creditor at the end of the year. It is a fundamental principle of modern tax law that, generally, tax calculations will follow good accounting practice unless there is a rule of tax law in a particular area that overturns or contradicts those practices and principles.

Similarly, other expenses which arise over time, or in relation to specific periods, for example rentals and rates, can be regarded in some instances as accruing on a day-to-day basis, so that the appropriate proportion has to be charged in the P&L account for a particular period even though the expenses may have yet to be paid.

It is thus of crucial importance to the proper preparation of financial statements, and hence the correct calculation of the tax liable profits of a business, that your records are detailed and adequate to enable your accountant to properly reflect all accrued expenses therein and to identify which expenses need to be properly treated as creditors at the end of the financial year. Otherwise your taxable profits may end up being higher than they need to be.

A step further along this road is asking yourself, as the year end approaches, what expenses the business has coming up shortly and whether or not incurring any of these prior to the end of the financial year will defer tax liabilities significantly. If your expenses can be accelerated slightly, this might be rewarding as you may be able to defer liabilities for a whole year. An example might be identifying any specific repairs or maintenance costs which you are planning to carry out in the near future. A short acceleration in timing might only affect your cash flow slightly but could significantly accelerate the tax deduction for these expenses from one year to the earlier one. Clearly the commercial drivers of your business are of paramount importance, but bringing forward expenses by a short period of time so that liabilities are deferred for a long period of time can impact the tax relief you receive and how soon your business tax bills arise.

Income recognition

A strategic approach should also be taken with income recognition. Here, expert advice should be sought. There are specific rules and accounting standards which apply to the recognition of income, especially for stock valuations, recognition of the value of work-in-progress, long-term contract work, when professional services should be recognised as completed and hence billable services, and so on. All these rules have to be properly followed.

It is important to pay close attention to the annual and seasonal patterns of trading and as the financial year end approaches it should be ensured that no unnecessary acceleration of the recognition of income is occurring in the financial accounts. For example, a hotel business receiving deposits this year for next year should normally account for those as income of the following year not in the year of receipt. It is important to ensure that the business accounting systems recognise this difference accurately so that taxable profits are not accelerated incorrectly.

Business expenses

Expenditure reliefs

When your business incurs an expense you may expect that you can get tax relief on it. However, not all expenses may actually be relieved against profits for tax purposes. There are two fundamental principles involved here:

1. An expense must be a *revenue expense* and not a *capital expense* for it to be deductible against your business profits.

2. An expense must be incurred *wholly and exclusively for the purposes of the trade or business.*

1. Revenue expenses and capital expenses

A *revenue expense* is an ordinary everyday cost of running a business – an inevitable and essential expense. It is also one that does not involve the acquisition, creation or improvement of some new or existing capital asset or an advantage that will endure for the benefit of business.

Capital expenditure is not an allowable deduction against business profits but instead it goes on the balance sheet as an asset; this is an established basic accounting concept. Thus, buying vehicles, office furniture or buildings does not attract tax relief directly through the P&L account. Some of these types of expenditure may attract tax relief via the separate capital allowances system for commercial depreciation as discussed earlier, but otherwise they are non-deductible.

Let's take a look at an example of how revenue and capital expenses differ.

Refurbishments to buildings: repairs and improvements

It is very important to recognise which types of costs will get your business a tax deduction from the outset. For example, when you are considering carrying out a refurbishment of a building you need to recognise that repair costs attract tax relief but improvement costs do not. All too often where property projects are concerned the person preparing the accounts and tax calculations is left to deal with inadequate paperwork after the event. Commonly this results in less tax relief being achieved than should have

> **When considering carrying out a refurbishment of a building remember that repair costs attract tax relief but improvement costs do not.**

been the case because the documentary evidence was not planned in detail before the project started. Thus identifying precisely what is being done and getting it properly identified on suppliers' and subcontractors' invoices is of the utmost importance.

Of course it is perhaps arguable that every repair cost has some element of improvement in it – every repair is an improvement in the sense that what you have done is make something better – but this does not mean that the expense does not get tax relief. The important consideration is whether wear-and-tear caused over the years is being fixed or whether something new is being added that was not there before.

Thus if your factory's roof leaks like a sieve, getting it fixed is a repair and genuinely tax deductible, no matter how much it costs. Even if you take the whole roof off and replace it with a brand new one this is still a repair. However, if at the same time you take the opportunity to raise the roof ten feet so that the attic space now becomes usable business space where it was not before, then arguably the purpose of the expense has become a capital one. You might be able to convince HMRC inspector that some repairs element should be allowed against your profits (such compromises are common and should be sought where possible) but strictly the character of the expense has changed to a capital one.

Other examples of repairs versus improvements:

- Resurfacing a roadway would normally be a simple repair but putting a new tarmac surface down on top of a new hard core base instead of simply replacing an old gravel surface would probably be regarded as a capital improvement.

- Replacing old earthen pipes underneath a builder's yard with new plastic piping would probably be regarded as a capital improvement and not a repair.

- Installing a steel security fence around a yard to replace an old wooden panel fence would be regarded as a capital improvement and not a repair.

2. Business expenses versus personal expenses

Unincorporated businesses

The proprietor of an unincorporated business needs to be aware that a second restriction might be relevant on whether or not tax relief can be obtained for an expense. (Those operating through limited companies still have to calculate this potential effect but in a somewhat different manner, as will be covered later.)

If you run a business on your own as a sole trader or in partnership then you need to be alert to what happens when you spend money on yourself as opposed to on the business. These sort of costs are not generally tax deductible. They are *drawings* from the business. Personal expenses of the proprietor therefore need to be recorded separately from the running costs of the business.

Problems will potentially arise where an expense has both a business and a private motive, most commonly for example motoring and travel expenses. If the freelance IT consultant drives 250 miles to a customer's premises then normally this will be allowable for tax purposes. If he makes a personal call along the way this should not turn what is primarily a business journey into primarily a private one, but it does undoubtedly turn it into a dual purpose trip. Strictly this would mean that the costs are no longer tax deductible as they do not meet the statutory *wholly and exclusively* test. In practice HMRC will in fact accept that a portion of such an expense can be claimed against profits provided the proprietor makes an objective assessment each year of the private element of such expenses.

HMRC will not normally countenance an attempt to disguise personally motivated costs as business expenses. For example, it is common to see businesses donating money to local sports clubs or teams. Whether this is done out of personal preference or in a genuine attempt to create business goodwill and advertising is debatable in many cases. The personal motivations of a business owner are arguably often inextricably linked with their business in their own minds.

You need to have a clear view of why an expense is being incurred and it is important to be able to identify a primary business purpose for any expenses. If there is a mixed or dual purpose it will be of even more importance to be able to demonstrate that any personal purpose was merely *incidental* to the primary business reason for incurring the expense. It may be possible, for instance, to demonstrate that the personal element was a benefit which arose as a mere incidental feature of the business purpose, in which case it will probably be arguable that all of the costs should be treated as tax deductible.

Limited companies

When your business is run through a limited company any personal expenses incurred and paid for by the company will normally be charged to your director's personal loan account. So long as this is in credit there is no problem. If it goes overdrawn then there will be tax charges to pay by both the company and you personally on this *benefit in kind*, i.e. the overdrawn amount will be treated as a beneficial loan. If the company pays personal expenses on behalf of employees or provides them with any other sort of benefit then there will normally be a tax liability on these persons.

In this sort of situation the *wholly and exclusively* test should not normally be an issue with a company, unless the expense is so far removed from either remunerating you personally, or so distant from the company's trade, that it cannot under any perspective be regarded as a business expense. For example, if your company pays for the costs of a car for a member of your family and the company decides that this is simply another part of your overall remuneration package then this should mean that these costs continue to be tax deductible for your company. This will, however, result in a taxable benefit on you personally and you will need to weigh up carefully whether or not the real income tax and NIC costs of this are worthwhile overall.

Identify and record expenses correctly

It should be clear from the above that it is important to properly identify which expenses relate to your business and which do not. Disputes between businesses and HMRC may arise where records are not adequate to properly differentiate expenses and also where there is confusion over the boundary between business and non-business expenses. You should put a sound and accurate record-keeping system in place, keep personal and private expenses separate, ensure that expenses you incur personally on behalf of your business are recorded in detail and itemise all business expenses carefully.

> " Disputes between businesses and HMRC may arise where records are not adequate to properly differentiate private from business expenses and also where there is confusion over the boundary between business and non-business expenses. "

With the user-friendly computerised accounting systems available nowadays there is little excuse for not recording expenses in detail.

Of course you must also have documentation in the form of receipts and vouchers so that if your records are ever the subject of a compliance check by HMRC they can be shown that you know what you are doing and are controlling your costs efficiently.

Home expenses

The proprietor of an unincorporated business may be able to claim relief for a variety of other expenses, specifically perhaps those incurred in working from home. Where a room is set aside for business use then a proportion of the overhead costs of running the property may be legitimately claimed as genuine business costs and deducted against the annual profits. Care should be taken here and specific tax advice will be necessary, as in these circumstances there is always the risk that HMRC might seek to charge CGT on a proportion of the otherwise normally exempt private residence when it is sold. This is actually quite rare in practice but it needs to be borne in mind.

If a room is to be set aside in this manner then the expense claim should be prepared on an objective basis using a formulaic approach to the apportionment of the expenses, ideally by reference to the area of the room and also by reference to the actual business use of it as opposed to the degree of personal use as well.

It should also be remembered that there may be legal restrictions on the use of a property for a business purpose and this may also affect the validity of household insurance policies. There may also be local bye-laws to be taken into account.

Where the business is run through a limited company you may find it much more difficult to claim for these sort of costs – indeed this is one reason why many small businesses should consider carefully the pros and cons of incorporation as it can lead to the loss of the ability to claim these costs against taxable profits. You might consider having the company rent space in your own

6. Business Tax Bills

property from you for the purposes of the business. However, the likelihood is that this would simply be giving the company a tax deduction, only for the rentals paid to you to be taxed as your income and so the whole process may not be worthwhile. A tax adviser or accountant would be able to advise you on the relative merits of such a strategy, in particular a review of the relative tax effects of the deduction available to the company and the marginal income tax effect on you personally will be necessary and will show whether this will be a good idea.

Capital allowances and timing issues

The tax regime includes a number of specific tax allowances such as capital allowances for plant and machinery (as discussed in chapter 2). Getting the most out of these available reliefs is important and will rest on having a clear understanding of what is and what is not qualifying expenditure and also being aware that timing issues can be important.

Expenditure will attract tax relief via the capital allowances system if it meets the criteria of one of the eligible categories; for example plant and machinery allowances, integral features, computer software, etc. For instance, it is important to ensure that the business has bought plant which qualifies for the 100% Enhanced Capital Allowances available for energy efficient plant rather than plant that only qualifies for a much lower rate of allowances, perhaps only 20% (18% from April 2012). Whenever a business is contemplating a purchase of new plant it will be a good idea to review the qualifying categories (detailed at **www.eca.gov.uk**) that bring eligibility for these higher rates of allowances.

There are many case law judgements on these various definitions of plant and machinery, and if in doubt you will need to consult a specialist tax adviser to assist you on whether or not a particular item of expenditure may attract tax relief. In most cases, especially where buildings or structure purchases are concerned, the expertise of specialist valuers or quantity surveyors in apportioning costs will be important.

Even so, in a large number of cases the deciding factor in maximising capital allowances claims is not specific expertise on interpreting clever and innovative case law decisions, but rather it is detailed analysis work and cost allocations among the main categories such as structural costs, integral or loose plant, fixtures and fittings, and plant and equipment. A lot of tax relief is commonly lost because someone fails to put in place at the start of a project accurate and detailed cost accounting and reporting systems which would enable the tax adviser to prepare adequately detailed tax calculations after the project is finished.

Identify the date on which expenditure is incurred

The date on which expenditure is incurred is crucial for establishing entitlement to capital allowances in one accounting period or another. Contract terms will normally establish the date on which an unconditional obligation to pay is incurred and this is when entitlements to capital allowances arises.

There are special rules for periods of credit, and longer term what are known as milestone contracts, and these will need to be reviewed carefully when such contracts are being used. Clearly if a large plant purchase is being planned then whether or not the tax relief is going to become available in the current accounting period or the next is an important consideration for any business. If you can get the tax relief sooner rather than later then this will probably be preferable. Furthermore, when available rates of tax relief change – for instance the fall from 40% First Year Allowances to only 20% annual allowances that was bought in on 31 March 2010 – getting the expenditure in before the rate drops will be preferable, if practical.

Delivery and ownership terms

Paying close attention to contract terms, delivery terms and the legalities of equipment purchases may enable a business to significantly affect its overall tax liability in a particular financial period. A contract establishing that a business has an unconditional obligation to pay for plant which is dated 29 March and must pay for the plant within, say, 30 days, will establish entitlement to capital allowances on that date. So if

> **"** Paying close attention to contract terms, delivery terms and the legalities of equipment purchases may enable a business to significantly affect its overall tax liability in a particular financial period. **"**

the business' accounting year ends on 31 March then the capital allowances are available this year and not in the next one.

In some cases structuring plant purchases via deferred payment or hire purchase contract terms will also enable the capital allowances available to be accelerated and this should clearly be considered if at all possible.

Identify available special reliefs

The capital expenditure relief systems in force in the UK also offer businesses some other reliefs such as Research and Development (R&D) allowances. There is also the related tax credits system, under which a small company can obtain an extra 75% tax relief on qualifying expenditures.

Where a company is incurring these types of cost it is well worth a close look to see if it might qualify for special reliefs as these can be a very effective way of reducing overall taxable profits. Special reliefs are not all that easy to obtain and sometimes it requires some work to convince HMRC that the relief is indeed due, but the amounts of tax relief at stake can be very significant indeed and it will often be worthwhile investing in specialist advice to secure these reliefs help. HMRC specialists will often offer assistance and guidance on the formulation of such claims, for example on R&D Reliefs.

Involving the family

Everyone has tax allowances and tax thresholds. This includes a personal tax allowance to offset taxable income and a basic rate tax band available before income tax must be paid at the higher rates. Since 5 April 2010 individuals earning £100,000 and above will progressively lose their personal tax allowance. Once income rises above £112,950 individuals are not entitled to a personal tax allowance at all. This threshold will rise to £114,950 from 6 April 2011.

There is sometimes the possibility that the taxable profits of a business might be reduced by involving more family members in the running of the business and hence using some of their personal tax allowances against those profits.

Let's take an example of a family farming partnership consisting of four individuals; mother, father and two sons. They all work in the business and all share in the profits. It is therefore

> **❝** There is tax case law precedent for dealing with cases where individuals have sought to deduct such wages for the employment of family members where the amounts paid were regarded as excessive for the work undertaken. **❞**

obvious that their personal tax allowances and basic rate threshold bands can be used to offset the personal taxable incomes. This means that the income tax liability on this business' profits will be less than the tax payable by a sole trader earning the same level of profits.

However, a subtly different situation is where a proprietor of a business employs family members to deliberately reduce the overall tax burden. This is a controversial area and should be approached with considerable caution. What is clear is that when someone, for example a spouse, works as an employee in a business and genuinely does work for the business then it is perfectly reasonable to pay him or her a wage commensurate with the work done and to obtain tax relief for that wage. Personal tax allowances will be available against that wage and the basic rate tax band will be available for any wages above the level of the personal tax allowance.

Of course, where wages or salaries paid to family members exceed the statutory thresholds then PAYE tax and NICs will have to be operated in accordance with PAYE regulations.

There is tax case law precedent for dealing with cases where individuals have sought to deduct such wages for the employment of family members where the amounts paid were regarded as excessive for the work undertaken. This is not acceptable and will fail the *wholly and exclusively* test mentioned earlier. For instance, tax relief cannot be obtained for money being handed over to children as their normal pocket money. Indeed, employing minors in your business is inherently risky and is likely to attract the attention of HMRC.

Here again, though, the nature of your business should be considered. In some industries, such as agriculture, the employment of family members is customary so modest wages for work actually done will be acceptable. Be aware of the national minimum wage legislation which should be taken into account.

Use of pensions

Pensions represent one of the most abiding and effective means of reducing personal tax bills. There are very few financial products available which currently offer 40% income tax relief, or full relief against CT profits. Wherever someone contributes to a pension scheme it is likely that their taxable income can be reduced by the amount of those pension contributions.

Under provisions contained in the 2009 Finance Act, tax relief for pensions contributions for individuals whose income exceeds £150,000 is to be heavily curtailed from 5 April 2011, and additional forestalling provisions have been brought in to prevent such individuals seeking to put large contributions into their pensions in the years before this new set of rules comes into effect.

Contributions by employers to employees' pension funds are also potentially to be taxed on the pension fund holder where the contributions in the future exceed set thresholds (currently set between £20,000 and £30,000 depending upon the pattern of previous contributions to the scheme). This most recent attack on pensions has put something of a dampener on the attractiveness of pensions at the upper end of the income scale, but for many business owners they represent a significant means of reducing the effective rates of tax on business profits. These proposals may be subject to change again before April 2011.

For the limited company there remains the prospect that significant taxable profits can be removed from the charge to tax by the making of pensions contributions which can be deducted against the company's taxable profits.

The use of Small Self-Administered Schemes (SASS) for owner-managed companies has been popular for many years and provides what can be a very flexible vehicle for use in tax planning in conjunction with the company structure. For example, a company looking to buy a new office block might consider whether in fact its pension fund might be a suitable vehicle to fund the ownership of the office block. Contributions to the pension fund could attract tax relief against company profits and then the pension fund could buy the property. In this manner the company would in effect get full 100% tax relief on the purchase of its property, something that otherwise would be impossible.

Of course anyone contemplating setting up a pension scheme or using one to assist in their tax planning will need to seek specialist financial and investment advice from someone properly authorised to practice in that field. Tax relief is not always the first consideration when a pension scheme is being set up, but if properly used in conjunction with expert advice pensions can represent a tax effective vehicle.

Summary

- Review and ensure compliance with generally accepted accounting principles (GAAP).

- Put good record-keeping systems in place.

- Ensure correct identification of revenue expenditures.

- Pay close attention to timing rules for expenditures.

- Claim all available capital allowances.

- Consider special regimes for expenditures that may be available.

- Identify all *use of home* expenses that can be claimed.

- Consider involving family members as taxpayers where appropriate.

- Use pensions schemes where practical to do so.

7. Personal Tax Bills

Introduction

When running a business you need to give careful consideration to how you take profits out of it. To a large extent this is dictated by the choices you make initially about your business structure.

Extracting funds from a limited company is arguably more difficult and potentially more costly than extracting funds from a sole tradership or partnership. However, as we have already seen, the overall tax rate and tax liabilities can be significantly lower using a limited company. Whichever way you run your business the method by which you choose to pay yourself will have an impact on your personal tax liabilities and is therefore a fundamental part of your tax planning strategy.

Income tax bands 2010-11	
Personal allowance (no income tax payable on income below this level)	£6,475
Basic rate (20%)	£6,476-£37,400
Higher rate (40%)	£37,401-£150,000
Additional rate (50%)	Over £150,000

For more information see: **www.hmrc.gov.uk/rates/it.htm**

Review the alternative ways of paying yourself

Drawings by sole traders and partners

The proprietor of an unincorporated business can take *drawings* from their business without incurring an immediate tax charge. This is because their tax bills are calculated on their annual profits, not on the occasion of actually extracting funds from the business.

However, when you draw funds from such a business you need to be alert to the correlation between these funds and the profits you make. If you overdraw your personal capital account with the business then some of the interest payable on the business bank account, and some of the related bank charges, might have to be regarded as private expenses (they would almost certainly be regarded in this way by HMRC) and so would have to be disallowed in computing the taxable business profits, thus resulting in higher tax bills. As you draw funds from your business you should therefore always ensure that you put funds aside to pay your eventual income tax bills. To do this you or your accountants will need to prepare a careful forecast of the business' expected profitability and the potential tax liabilities that will then flow from those profits.

The proprietor of the unincorporated business arguably has a greater degree of flexibility in dealing with dual-purpose expenses (as discussed in the last chapter). Where an expense is part business/part private then strictly there should be no deduction against your business profits. However, over many years it has become customary for HMRC to accept that expenses which have a primarily business purpose, such as travel or similar, can be deducted against business profits if they are subjected to an objectively quantified private use adjustment.

In some cases, therefore, the proprietor of an unincorporated business might perceive that they can obtain tax relief on partially private expenses which they could otherwise not achieve using a different structure. Care needs to be taken to ensure that this flexibility is not abused and that tax relief is only claimed for expenses with a primarily business purpose and merely an incidental private motive, so as to ensure that the expense is not disallowed in its entirety.

You should decide from the outset how much you will draw from your business on a regular basis. This will probably be best done by setting up a standing order from the business bank account to your private bank account. You should then set aside some of this money for the related income tax and NIC liabilities which you will have to pay when your self-assessment return is submitted to HMRC.

Limited companies – the shareholders' earnings

If you run your business through a limited company then you have to remember that whenever you pay yourself there is a potential immediate tax and possibly NIC consequence because you and the company are legally separate persons.

You can choose to pay yourself a salary on a regular monthly or weekly basis. This will need to be in excess of the national minimum wage (NMW) if you have a proper service contract with your own company. The NMW regulations apply to workers engaged on a contract of employment and currently this rule seems to be interpreted quite literally. Thus if your company does not give you a written contract then it is debatable whether or not the NMW rules apply to you personally. There are also exceptions for family run businesses in some circumstances. Be aware that HMRC enforces the NMW rigorously.

If your regular salary exceeds the PAYE income tax and NICs threshold in force for a tax year then you will need to operate PAYE on the salary and make monthly payments of tax and NICs to HMRC of these deductions. The company will also need to pay

Employers' NICs on your salary, at 12.8% on all payments to you (rising to 13.8% from April 2011).

If it has sufficient profits the company can also pay bonuses at intervals during the financial year in order to top-up the pay of directors or other employees. Again, however, this will be subject to deductions of PAYE income tax and NICs from both these people and the company.

A shareholder in a company can also receive dividends out of the profits of that company, so long as it actually has profits to pay out as dividends. If there are no profits then it is illegal to pay any dividends (indeed they may have to be repaid to the company in these circumstances).

When paying yourself from your own limited company, then, it is important to choose the right mix of salary, bonuses and dividends. Many small company owner-managers currently pay themselves a fairly small salary and then dividends at intervals throughout the year. This is in order to take advantage of the currently favourable way in which dividends are taxed below the higher rate income tax threshold and also their favourable status for NIC purposes.

Drawing money from the business with dividends

The current UK regime taxes dividends at the lower rate of 10% where the individual's total taxable income falls below the higher rate income tax threshold. For tax years 2010/2011 this threshold is set at £43,875 – the personal allowance of £6,475 plus the basic rate tax band of £37,400. This, in effect, means that the recipient of a dividend suffers no income tax at all because dividends come with a non-repayable tax credit of 10% and so are regarded as having been taxed at source.

Thus a net dividend received of £900 is equivalent to gross taxable income of £1000, the tax credit being £100 (one-ninth of the net dividend or 10% of the gross distribution). The company will of course have paid CT on these profits before the dividend is paid out to you and for small companies (profits below £300,000 in most cases) this is at 21% for tax year 2010, falling to 20% from 2011.

Where an individual's total income exceeds the basic rate tax threshold then their dividends are taxed as the *top slice* of their income. If the dividend slice crosses the threshold then only that part of the gross dividend which is above the threshold attracts the special higher rate of income tax applicable to dividends, currently set at 32.5%. For dividends above the new £150,000 income threshold introduced on 6 April 2010, the rate of tax is 42.5%.

Further to this, dividends are not currently liable to any NICs.

Despite the expectations of many tax advisers and commentators, HMRC has not so far shown itself especially willing to challenge the use of this low salary-high dividend strategy. Legislation does exist to facilitate such a challenge in both the income tax and the NICs codes if

> **"The current UK income tax regime only taxes dividends at the lower rate of 10% where the individual's total taxable income falls below the higher rate income tax threshold. "**

HMRC were so minded. This is an area that is possibly subject to change in the future, so advice should be sought from your accountant when deciding whether to pay yourself more in salary or in dividends throughout the year.

Practicalities of payment through dividends

If you decide to adopt this strategy for your company it is essential that you take some basic administrative actions. You should ensure that:

- You have good management accounts that support the payment of dividends.

- Your company can legally vote dividends.

- Dividends are properly voted and minuted in the company books.

- The company secretarial work necessary for proper dividend voting is completed properly and at the right time.

Failure to take the above steps can lead to compliance errors and may even lead to the dividends being regarded as illegal for Company Law and tax purposes with potentially very costly results for both you and the company.

There is an important choice to be made here. If the profits are extracted from your limited company as dividends not salary then the company will first have to pay CT on the profits it has made. Only profits after CT has been paid are eligible to be paid out as dividends.

Thus a company earning taxable profits of £60,000 in its accounting period ending 31 March 2010 will have to pay 21% CT (£12,600) leaving £47,400 available to pay out to the shareholders as dividends. If this company were to pay all these profits out to the proprietor as salary there would be considerable NIC liabilities to pay on top of the income tax due on these earnings.

Let's look at an example of how this might work.

Example 6 – payment through salary

Evelyn operates as a freelance family guidance counsellor and her limited company makes profits of £60,000 for the year to 31 March 2011. If she pays out all of this profit as salary, including NIC payable by the company, this will leave her with cash in her hands of £37,683.88. This is calculated as follows.

Employer's NICs

Company profits	£60,000
Salary (grossed up for Employer's NICs at 12.8%)	£60,000 x (100/112.8) = £53,191
Employer's NICs	£60,000 - £53,191 = £6,809

Profits liable to CT this year are therefore reduced to £0 because the salary and NICs are fully tax deductible against the company's profits for CT purposes.

Employee's NICs (see figures for class 4 NICs on p. 84)

Salary (£53,191/12)	£4,432.58 per month
£0-£476 per month	No NIC payable
£476-£3,656 per month NIC payable at 11%	(£3,656 - £476 = £3,180) £3,180 at 11% = £349.80
£3,657-£4,432.58 per month NIC payable at 1%	(£4,432.58 - £3,657 = £775.58) £775.58 at 1% = £7.76
Total NIC payable per month	£349.80 + £7.76 = £357.56
Total NIC payable for the year	£357.56 x 12 = £4,290.72

Employee's tax calculations

Employee's income tax salary	£53,191
Deduct personal tax allowance	£6,475
Taxable salary £53,191 - £6,475	£46,716
Portion taxed at 20% is £37,400	£37,400 x .20 = £7,480
Portion taxed at 40% is £9,316 (£46,716 - £37,400)	£9,316 x .40 = £3,726.40
Total income tax for the year	£7,480 + £3,726.40 = £11,206.40

Disposable cash remaining

Salary	£53,191
NIC	£4,290.72
Tax	£11,206.40
Total cash left to Evelyn	£53,181 - £4,290.72 - £11,206.40 = £37,683.88

This is an effective tax rate of 37% on profits of £60,000.

Example 7 – payment through dividends

If Evelyn decided to pay herself a small salary, to use up her personal income tax allowance for the year (which is £6,475), and then pay the balance out as dividends instead of salary, the position would alter as follows.

Company profits	£60,000
Salary paid out to Evelyn	£6,475
Company profits liable to corporation tax	£60,000 - £6,475 = £53,525
Corporation due at 21% for this year	£53,525 x .21 = £11,240.25
Company retained profits before dividends	£53,525 - £11,240.25 = £42,284.75
Dividends paid out to shareholders	£42,284
Profits retained inside the company	£nil

The net dividend payment of £42,284 is treated as equivalent to 90% of gross income because dividends are regarded as having paid 10% tax at source. This then gives a gross distribution to the shareholder for tax purposes of £46,982 ([£42,284/90] x 100).

This is regarded as income received net of a tax credit deduction at 10%, which is available to set against any higher rate income tax liability, but is not repayable to the shareholder under any circumstances. Thus on this dividend and salary mix Evelyn's income tax liability would be as follows.

Income tax liability

Salary	£6,475
Dividend (gross)	£46,982
Gross income	£6,475 + £46,982 = £53,457
Tax payable at 0% on £6,475	£0
Tax payable at 10% on £37,400	£3,740
Tax payable at 32.5% on £9,582	£3,114
Less tax credits	£4,698
Net tax to pay	£2,156

The tax credits shown above represent the difference between the gross distribution £46,982 and the net dividend £42,284. These are notional credits, not available for repayment to the shareholder but available for set off against any higher rate income tax liability which the shareholder may incur on the gross distribution of £46,982.

Additionally there would be about £84 of employee's NICs due on the small salary, giving total tax and NICs of £2,240 on profits of £60,000.

Disposable cash remaining

Salary	£6,475
Dividend (net)	£42,284
Dividend (gross)	£46,982
Tax	£2,156
NIC	£84
Total cash left to Evelyn	£46,982 - £2,156 - £84 = £44,742

This gives an effective tax rate of 25%, which is clearly preferable to using the salary route in Example 6. This serves to illustrate that there are very significant tax and NIC savings to be made simply from the choice the owner-manager makes about how to remunerate himself or herself out of the profits of their business. Using the dividends route extra disposable cash of £7,058 (or £588 per month) would be available to Evelyn.

Another interesting comparison is to look at the income tax and class 4 NICs liability that Evelyn would suffer if this £60,000 profit had been earned in an unincorporated business.

Example 8 – an unincorporated business

Income tax

Profits	£60,000
Tax payable at 0% on £6,475	£0
Tax payable at 20% on £37,400	£7,480
Tax payable at 40% on £16,125	£6,450
Total	£7,480 + £6,450 = £13,930

Class 4 NICs (see figures for class 4 NICs on p. 84)

NICs payable at 8% on £38,160	£3,052.80
NICs payable at 1% on £16,125	£161.25
Total	£3,214.05

Evelyn would also have to pay Class 2 NIC's of £2.40 per week, which represents a total of £125 for the year.

Total income tax and NICs = £13,930 + £3,214.05 + £125 = £17,269

Thus Evelyn's disposable cash after tax and NIC would be £42,731 (£60,000 - £17,269), which is an effective tax rate of 29%. This is significantly higher than the liability using the limited company route with small salary and higher dividends.

Examples 6, 7 and 8 have shown that the means by which the proprietor extracts their profits from their business is an essential feature of the way their tax bills arise. The dividend/salary choice is one of many that managers of limited companies face.

Flexibility with expenses

The proprietor of an unincorporated business will have some additional flexibility with expenses when compared to those using a limited company. If you operate through a limited company you will have to choose how to deal with expenses you incur personally on behalf of your business.

For example, if you decide to run a car through the company which you use personally then you will have to pay income tax charges on the benefit in kind out of your take home salary or dividends each month. You will therefore probably need to ensure that the company pays you extra each month to enable you to fund this additional cost. Alternatively, you could run the car yourself but then the company will not get tax relief on all the vehicle running costs. I discuss this later in more detail.

If you run your business as a sole trader then there can be no question of taxable car benefits on you, as you are the proprietor of the business not a director or employee. This means that the costs of the vehicle can normally be charged through the business with very specific adjustment being made to reflect your private use of the vehicle over the tax year. Similar private use scale adjustments will have to be made if your business is liable to register for VAT and you reclaim the VAT input tax you pay on petrol and other vehicle running costs.

Optimise tax relief on borrowings

One of the key aspects of financing any business venture is arranging your borrowings. Ensuring that you will get tax relief on the costs of these borrowings is very important and optimising any other available tax relief on your personal borrowings should also be regarded as an important strategic objective. You should always bear in mind the possibility of getting tax relief on interest paid whenever you are using borrowed finance.

Care is needed as there are some provisions in place to prevent tax avoidance in this area, which can come into play if an individual engages in planning strategies that seek to obtain tax relief on manufactured or disguised interest. On the other hand, there is no specific provision which prevents you obtaining tax relief should you seek to finance your business in one manner rather than another. The way you finance your business is a personal choice to be discussed between you and your lender.

Only business interest is tax deductible

When a business pays interest on borrowed money and that interest is paid *wholly and exclusively* for the purposes of its trade then the borrowings will be regarded as business borrowings and the interest paid for the use of borrowed money will normally be treated as deductible against your business profits for tax purposes. If you have other private borrowings the interest on those will not normally attract tax relief unless those borrowings were specifically obtained to assist in financing the business.

Consider restructuring private borrowings

You should look closely at how both your personal and your business borrowings are structured to see if changes might make things more tax effective. Of course restructuring financing always relies on cooperation from your lenders, but if tax savings will accrue then this can often prove a persuasive negotiating tool where bankers are concerned.

Review how the business is financed

A profitable business means that your personal capital with the business is likely to gradually increase. The proprietor of an unincorporated business will have a capital account and if this stands at a healthy balance this means that you are financing the business with personal wealth. Owner-managers of limited companies often have a director's loan account with their company and similar considerations arise when this is in credit.

If you have a healthy balance owing to you from your business then drawing this out normally costs you personally nothing in tax. The business will incur a tax liability in earning any profits and thus accruing cash reserves in the business balance sheet, but if you then withdraw that money from your personal capital account with the business (be that a proprietor's capital account in a sole tradership or a director's loan account balance with your own limited company) this is the simple withdrawal of funds owing to you from the business and not an extraction of taxable earnings.

If the amounts involved are sizeable you may be able to use these funds to pay off personal borrowings. If this results in your business paying bank interest instead of you personally paying interest then this will reduce the taxable profits of the business. You will have replaced non-qualifying personal loan interest with tax deductible business interest, which is a sound move.

Personal expenses

Business tax deductions can normally only be obtained for expenses incurred wholly and exclusively for the purposes of the trade. Any personal expenses paid by the business must be clearly recorded as such so that when your accounts are prepared these can be charged against your capital account or company director's loan account and not treated as P&L expenses.

It may be worth looking closely at your personal expenditure profile to consider whether there are any costs you currently incur out of your personal taxed income which might qualify as business expenses. It is not permitted to disguise personal expenses as business expenses, but there may be costs which you can pay as tax deductible benefits to yourself as a company director or which can be paid as business expenses.

For example, let's think about the cost of sending a child to university. Earlier we looked at the possibility of employing family members and saw that this should approached with caution. If you can justify such a tactic because your child or family member does indeed work in the business then this might be a way of converting costs into allowable tax deductions.

> **It is not permitted to disguise personal expenses as business expenses, but there may be costs which you can pay as tax deductible benefits to yourself as a company director or which can be paid as business expenses.**

Tuition fees, for example, are in excess of £3,000 per annum and are set to rise further. If your daughter works for you during her holiday periods then the wages she receives might well be used by her to pay these tuition fees. This would effectively convert a cost you are currently paying out of your own taxed income into a tax deductible cost. Of course, you must ensure that the wages are properly due and paid to her for work actually done.

Similarly, imagine as the director of a company you are personally paying the costs of your son's car. A company car is a taxable benefit but some cars are not that tax-expensive these days. The tax system actively encourages businesses to purchase eco-friendly cars by reducing the taxable benefits charges. If your personal remuneration package is revised to include a benefit car which your son or daughter uses, you will personally suffer the income tax on it via your PAYE code, but the benefits charge on some cars is now as low as 10% of the list price.

This means a car costing £14,000 would give you personally an annual income tax charge of £1,400, which if you are a 40% taxpayer is £47 per month (£1,400 x 40% /12 = £47) plus about £180 per annum NICs payable by your company (£1,400 x 12.8%). So you and the business will suffer tax and NICs of £744 per annum for the benefit of being able to expense the costs of running this car through the business as a benefit for you.

The car is part of your remuneration package so there should really be no argument about the permissibility of the costs of running it through the company. It might be seen as a step too far to charge all the fuel to the business, but the other running costs should be deductible. Some might regard this as a rather provocative example of expenses structuring and you should consult with your tax advisers before embarking on such a strategy.

Let's look a little more at ways you might be able to refinance or restructure personal expenses to secure additional tax relief.

Loan interest

Take the example of someone running a buy-to-let property business financed with borrowed money. If you originally put down a 20% deposit to secure a buy-to-let mortgage this leaves you having some equity in the property. Your equity is simply a reflection of the financing choices you originally made about setting up that business and it is open to you to refinance the business to use up or access that equity.

HMRC's Business Income Manual comments on this in the context of rental businesses. In effect it tacitly acknowledges that if someone chooses to refinance their buy-to-let business to use up their historical equity in a particular property then the additional interest charges will become tax deductible against the rental income of their lettings business. For more detail see:

www.hmrc.gov.uk/manuals/bimmanual

So, if your property cost you £200,000 and you borrowed £160,000 using £40,000 of savings to cover the balance, then that £40,000 equity arguably still exists in the balance sheet of your property business.

One of the common features of the personal tax returns of many such business owners is that they often do not prepare a balance sheet when showing their rental income and profits on their personal self-assessment. Preparing such a balance sheet might well highlight this refinancing opportunity. You could refinance the property and take the newly borrowed £40,000 out of the lettings business to repay some of your private mortgage. You have converted non-tax relieved interest into tax deductible interest in one manoeuvre.

The HMRC's Business Income Manual even includes a recognition that someone who decides to rent out their own home on a buy-to-let basis and moves elsewhere may well be able to carry out a more comprehensive version of this tactic. If you put your home into such a buy-to-let business then its opening cost in the balance sheet can arguably be its market value at that date. If you then refinance the property and use the new borrowings to purchase another house or flat elsewhere, then this is simply a financing choice and the interest payable ought to be deductible against the rental profits, securing valuable tax relief.

Note that you could not extend this tactic by subsequently revaluing the property and then borrowing additional funds against that revalued property for personal use and then seek to gain tax relief on the interest referable to the revaluation portion of the new borrowings.

Tax relief is also available for interest paid on borrowings used to introduce funds to a trading business or to loan money to a trading business. For example, if you buy shares in an unquoted trading company using borrowed money then the interest on those borrowings is generally tax deductible against your general taxable income.

Similarly, if you borrow money to buy a share in a partnership carrying on a trade or to introduce working capital to such a business, or to make loans to an *unquoted* trading company, then again the interest on those borrowings is tax deductible against your general income.

One strategy that would take advantage of these provisions is possibly to arrange for one spouse to purchase shares in the family company from the other, using borrowed funds. The interest thereon should be tax deductible for the buying spouse against their total income and the selling spouse (who has no CGT liability because there are no such charges between spouses married and living together) may well be able to use those same funds to repay part or all of their personal mortgage. Again, this is a strategy on which you should take careful advice from your accountant or tax adviser.

Company cars

I have already discussed providing benefit cars for family members and the same tactic might be considered for a spouse who works in the business for only a modest wage. It is of course important to be able to demonstrate that the car represents a part of a reasonable and commensurate remuneration package.

A spouse who carries out some basic administrative tasks on behalf of your business might well need a car for the purposes of their job. If they are paid at only a modest rate then sometimes the numbers can work out quite beneficially for tax purposes.

An employee normally only pays income tax on the benefit of a car where the combined quantum of the benefit and the salary exceeds £8,500 per annum. Thus, someone receiving a salary of, say, £6,000 per annum and a car with a benefit computed at £2,000 per annum would not pay any income tax at all on the car benefit. Note that this will not be the case if the employee is a director as well! A car emitting less than 120 grams per kilometre of carbon dioxide is taxed at only 10% of the list price, so if the car costs less than £20,000 (list price) then there would arguably be no taxable benefit on the employee. Clearly it will be of the utmost importance to be able to demonstrate that this car is being provided for genuine employment reasons.

Of course if the proprietor of an unincorporated business making such a choice was also to use this employee's car, then HMRC might find this a little controversial and seek an additional private use adjustment in the business taxation computations. Clearly this would have to be the subject of an honest appraisal of the appropriate level of tax adjustment to make in your tax calculations when the annual self-assessment was done for the business.

Whenever you need a car for the purposes of your business you will need to consider carefully how this is to be financed. It is probably a more important consideration where you operate through a limited company as you will need to consider the benefit-in-kind tax and NIC charges. There are about 15 or so different variables to take into account in determining whether or not you should buy a new vehicle through your company or personally, ranging from the level of private and business mileage you will do each year, through the running and purchase costs of the car, your marginal personal tax rate and the company's CT rate and VAT position.

Consider using tax effective benefits in kind

The UK's comprehensive and complex regime for taxable benefits also needs to be borne in mind by proprietors of their own limited businesses. The example of the car for a family member illustrated some aspect of this.

Whenever the company provides you with a benefit or pays personal expenses on your behalf, a tax liability may arise. If the expenses are incurred by you in the ordinary course of your employment on behalf of your company, you may well be able to claim a matching expense tax deduction. Indeed if the expenses are clearly always going to be tax deductible then you should actively consider seeking a tax *dispensation* from the PAYE tax office your company is registered with so that you do not have to complete an annual benefits form (P11D) for them.

P11D forms can be a time consuming and unnecessary administrative procedure if there is going to be no tax for the HMRC to collect at the end of the process. HMRC will normally grant dispensations for such *in and out* expenses and you should always consider this as a possibility. It will entail you convincing the HMRC that your records are

> **Benefits and expenses are identified by HRMC as a significant tax compliance risk area.**

adequate to ensure that you are controlling such costs effectively and rigorously, but otherwise such dispensations are normally fairly straightforward to obtain.

Benefits and expenses are identified by HRMC as a significant tax compliance risk area, especially in family companies where the rules and regulations are often poorly understood. You should recognise that the provision of benefits and expenses by a company to its employees can trigger tax liabilities so these sort of costs do need to be identified and controlled carefully.

You should also put in place a proper petty cash control system to deal with day-to-day incidental expenses and ensure that a proper checking and control system is instigated and well understood by all your staff. Identify all benefits that your company is paying on your behalf and keep detailed records so that the annual tax reporting function can be dealt with properly and in a timely manner.

Tax relief on borrowings

In order to get the most out of tax reliefs on borrowings you should:

- Remember that only business interest is tax deductible.

- Review how the business is financed.

- Review personal expenses, e.g.

    - loan interest payments

    - company cars

Summary

- Review alternative business structures.

- Review how you will pay yourself.

- Consider the dividend alternative with an incorporated business.

- Review your borrowings.

- Review your personal expenditure items.

- Consider tax effective benefits and expenses.

8. Extracting Cash from a Business

Introduction

This chapter looks at the methods which limited companies and traders using unincorporated businesses may have available to them for extracting profits from their businesses and potential tax implications. It concentrates mainly on the limited company owner as most structures for the unincorporated business are relatively simple.

Extracting profits as a sole trader

The owner of an unincorporated business can take their profits out of their business at their own discretion and at any time (so long as there is money there to be taken) and there is normally no immediate tax consequence. Tax liabilities of the sole trader or partnership are paid in January and July each year and are self-assessed on the profits the business makes, not on how much money you have withdrawn from your business. Of course, as indicated earlier, if you overdraw the business' capital account then this can result in bank interest and charges being disallowable for tax deduction purposes. Furthermore, if you continually draw out profits that the business has not made then your cash position will rapidly deteriorate and you will end up going out of business.

Extracting profits from a company

The owner of the small limited company faces a more rigorous regulatory regime when it comes to taking profits out of the business. Any transactions between the director/shareholder and his or her company have a potential tax consequence which must be borne in mind. This applies whether you take cash, have the business pay personal expenses or liabilities on your behalf, or if the business transfers assets over to you as benefits.

If a company lends you money this has potential tax implications as well. A loan from a company can also have company law implications and should not be made without taking proper legal advice (although it is not uncommon to see the owners of small limited companies accidentally overdrawing their personal loan accounts with their companies with inevitable tax implications thereafter).

Use salary, dividends or benefits

The main options available to the company owner/shareholder are to extract profits as salary or bonuses, dividends, or benefits in kind.

Other possibilities are to consider the use of pension contributions in order to obtain tax relief on the profits being extracted from the company. A company might also pay rent to the owner of the proprietor of a property from which it trades. Additionally there are some expenses payments that can be made to company employees free of tax where these are regarded by HMRC as legitimate business expenses. Used judiciously these may be useful as part of an overall package of measures for extracting profits from the company. Of course the other option available to profitable companies is for the shareholder and owner of the company to simply leave some of the profits inside the company for a period of time rather than extract them and pay higher rates of income tax on these extractions.

Which is best; salary or dividends?

When a company director is paid a salary or bonuses at irregular intervals, the income tax implications need to be considered. You also need to take into account the affect on the company's overall CT position. For the individual whose company is earning good profits it is important to recognise that salary and the associated NIC costs attract a tax deduction for the company but also create a personal income tax liability on the recipient, and NIC liability on the recipient and paying company.

As discussed earlier, if you pay yourself a small salary every month your personal income tax allowance (via the PAYE code you have to operate against the salary) will be available to cover the taxable amounts. Thus if your salary was £500 per month in 2010/2011 you would have no income tax to pay as the personal allowance for that tax year is £6,475. There would, however, be some small NICs to pay as the starting threshold for the tax year is £476, so each month there would be employee's NICs to pay at 11% above the threshold of £2.64. The company would also have an employer's NIC liability of 12.8% on earnings between £476 and £500 (£24), which equates to £3.07 (£24 x (12.8/100)).

Using such a strategy the balance of the employee/director's earnings could be extracted as dividends (provided there are profits from which to pay them) – the tax and NIC implications of which we examined in chapter 7.

Accumulating profits

As your profits rise it is possible to retain them in the company and not extract them over the medium term. Obviously this depends to a large extent upon your personal expenditure needs and preferences – retaining profits inside the company will only be an option to the extent that they are surplus to your immediate requirements.

If you can afford to leave some profits inside your company then this might be a way of saving some tax over the longer term. However, it is important to recognise that sometimes this can have an effect on the availability of other capital tax reliefs. This is mainly because it might affect the *trading* status of your shares in the company for the purposes of some very valuable capital taxation reliefs (see chapters 10 and 11).

When a small company retains profits that have been subjected to tax at 21% (20% from April 2011), these reserves can stay in the company for as long as you wish. If they are subsequently extracted as bonuses or as dividends then the tax effects discussed in the examples in chapter 7 will arise. It will also be important to recognise, however, that accumulating very large cash reserves in the company, which are not obviously required as working capital, might lead to the HMRC coming to regard the company as an investment company with a consequent increase in the rate of CT to 28% that it is required to pay.

Retaining profits until the company ceases trading

It might be an option to retain these surplus profits until you wind the company up. If, for example, your company trades for a period of five years and each year you retain £20,000 of surplus profits inside the company rather than extracting them into your own hands, the result will be that the company ends up with a sizeable cash balance after a while.

Profits of £20,000 will suffer 21% (20% from April 2011) CT each year so that after five years the company will have accrued £79,000 cash reserves after tax has been paid. If at this stage you decide to close the company then any capital distributions you receive during the course of winding the company up will be treated as capital gains and not income. Capital distributions at this stage of a company's life can often qualify for a special tax relief known as entrepreneurs' relief, which can mean that the tax rate applied is 10%. I give more detail on this relief later.

Very often for small companies it is also possible to agree an informal winding up with HMRC so that the costs of a formal liquidation can be dispensed with. If, for example, costs were only £1,000 and the annual CGT exemption was £10,500 for the year in which the company was wound up, the CGT would probably be in the region of £6,650 taking the original costs to you of your shares as £1000. This is calculated as so:

```
(£79,000 - £1,000 - £1,000 - £10,500) x .1 (tax at 10%)
= £6,650
```

If you had extracted these surplus profits as salary or dividends over the years, the income tax and NIC costs would have been a lot higher – 40% income tax and 12.8% NICs for salary and 32.5% income tax on dividends (you would almost certainly have been a higher rate income taxpayer if you had decided on accumulating these profits over this period of time). So, as you can see, the tax savings will be in the region of 10% overall, which on these amounts is a large sum.

This does depend critically upon the trading status of the company. It has to be acknowledged that there is some risk that if a company scales down its activities and becomes little more than a money box then the 10% rate of tax on the capital gains resulting for the availability of the entrepreneurs' relief might well be in doubt. The CGT rate would then rise to 28% (if you are a higher rate taxpayer, under changes announced in the June 2010 Emergency Budget) and the advantages of retaining profits rather than extracting them would reduce to almost zero.

An extension of this strategy is to retain profits over a period of several years before the closing down and then starting up another company carrying on the same, or virtually the same, trading activities as the old one. However, HMRC might wish to challenge such a strategy as structured tax avoidance, especially if a succession of new companies were used to mitigate tax liabilities in this manner.

Review tax effective expenses and benefits

Your business may be able to pay for expenses or benefits on your behalf and sometimes this can be perceived as a useful means of extracting some of your profit from the business. For example, if you run a limited company most benefits are taxable on you as an employee. However, some benefits can be made available to you tax free or in a tax favoured form.

There are a range of tax-free benefits that employees can receive from their employer. The following is a list of some of the more important tax-free or tax favoured benefits that may be of use for limited companies:

- mobile telephones

- loans of bicycles and safety equipment

- free or subsidised meals at work

- pension or annuity costs met by the employer

- workplace nursery provision

- vouchers for nursery care

- travel expenses on business for directors of group companies and others

- retraining courses for employees on termination of employment

- long service awards paid as testimonials

- awards under suggestions schemes

- goodwill entertainment (corporate hospitality)

- small gifts received from third parties

- annual Christmas parties or the equivalent costing below £150 per head

- sports facilities for employees and families

- some relocation expenses

- pensions or lump sums on retirement or death

- employee liability insurance

- provision of security assets

- company vans where private use is prohibited except for journeys to and from home to work

- company minibuses seating nine or more employees

HMRC booklet IR480 gives full details on the various rules and procedures surrounding these benefits and also a range of other benefits and their tax implications. There is also a detailed A to Z summary of HMRCs rules and procedures for dealing with the whole range of taxable and tax free benefits on their website (**www.hmrc.gov.uk/paye/exb/a-z**).

Benefits should not be overlooked as part of the overall package of earnings that you can take from your company; you should always ensure that you take advantage of any cost that the company can pay on your behalf which is treated in a tax favoured way under the benefits rules.

> **You should always ensure that you take advantage of any cost that the company can pay on your behalf which is treated in a tax favoured way under the benefits rules.**

A good example of this is the availability of tax approved mileage allowances where you use your own car on company business. The company can pay you up to 40p per mile (up to the first 10,000 miles) and 25p per mile thereafter free of any tax and NICs. There are also a range of other mileage allowances for using your own car or a company car which can be received tax free. Details can be found at **www.hmrc.gov.uk/rates/travel.htm**.

Expenses in an unincorporated business

For the owner of an unincorporated business the payment of personal expenses through the business is less complex. Private benefits and expenses paid for by the business should be treated as *drawings* and not charged against profits. Where the expense is primarily a business one with perhaps some incidental private element then it can legitimately be charged to profits with an objectively quantified private use adjustment being made in the annual taxation computations.

Pension contributions

Pensions have long been a tax favoured investment in the UK, attracting relief at an individual's marginal rate of income tax where pensions are paid for personally and attracting a deduction against profits where paid for by an employer. For very high earners this is to change from 2011, with the introduction of a new tax regime for those earning over £150,000 per annum. Under these new rules such individuals will no longer be able to obtain higher rate income tax relief on their pension payments and contributions to their funds by their employer may also attract a punitive income tax charge. At the time of writing these provisions are to be the subject of further detailed review.

For small business owners pension contributions will remain one of the few tax favoured investments which are available as a means of reducing overall tax liabilities and so this is an area to which you should certainly pay attention. Indeed, there are no other investments of a similar type available that offer the higher rate taxpayer this sort of tax deductible expense.

> " For small business owners pension contributions will remain one of the few tax favoured investments which are available as a means of reducing overall tax liabilities. "

Of course investments can go down as well as up, but the tax benefits of personal pension schemes are significant and represent a very popular method of reducing overall personal tax liabilities. The corollary is that once paid into the pension scheme the funds are difficult to access except in very tightly constrained circumstances, generally not until retirement and even then there are strict rules about how much can be drawn out of pension funds and when.

When investigating pensions you should always seek advice from a professionally qualified expert – as with any financial investment.

Pensions in unincorporated businesses

The self-employed individual sole trader or partner in a partnership can effectively pay personal pension contributions up to the level of their total relevant taxable earnings in a tax year. There are annual and lifetime caps on the amounts that can be paid into such personal pensions but these are set relatively high and are unlikely to be relevant. For example, the annual allowance for tax year 2009-10 as set at £245,000 with a lifetime allowance set at £1,750,000. It is likely that this annual allowance regime will be heavily curtailed from April 2011 under the results of a consultation and review process announced in the 2010 Emergency Budget.

Pensions in incorporated businesses

The owner-manager of a limited company has different pension options, including the ability to use personal pensions or to set up an occupational pension scheme through the company. Subject to specific rules and constraints company contributions to pension schemes normally attract direct tax relief as a deduction against company profits. However, those restrictions only tend to come into play when profits are very large and hence where the desired pension contributions are consequently large as well.

Subject to HMRC approval and contributions limits, any amount that a small company pays into a pension on behalf of its directors should attract direct tax relief against the company's profits. This therefore represents a very direct method of extracting profits from the company in a tax deductible manner. The added benefit is that any funds invested in the company's pension

> **"**Subject to HMRC approval and contributions limits, any amount that a small company pays into a pension on behalf of its directors should attract direct tax relief against the company's profits, **"**

scheme will be invested there free of tax on any investment income. For example, if the pension fund earns interest or invests in rental property these earnings will roll up inside the pension fund free of taxation for the term of the pension fund itself.

Furthermore, if the pension fund invests in assets which grow in value then any eventual disposals of those assets will normally be free of CGT inside the pension fund as well. This facility is sometimes combined with the desire to transfer ownership of property inside a company to a pension fund.

For example, the opportunity might be taken to sell the company's offices or business premises to the pension fund. This might trigger chargeable gains liable to CT inside the company, but if the gains are not too large and the tax liability can be managed this might be a good tactic to remove future growth in the value of the property from the scope of taxation altogether.

Contributions to the pension fund would be needed to endow it with the funds to make the purchase but these could be provided in the form of tax deductible contributions from the company itself. Thereafter the company could rent the property from the pension fund and receive an annual deduction against its profits for the rents paid and the rents would also roll-up free of taxation inside the pension fund.

Structured tax planning

The use of an Employee Benefit Trust (EBT) is another tax planning technique available to companies. These are specially designed tax planning structures set up to receive funds from companies for the payment of benefits to the company's employees. The company seeks a tax deduction against its profits for CT in respect of the contributions it makes to the trust. Once the funds have been paid into the trust the trustees can then consider paying benefits to company employees. There are strict rules for income tax and CT purposes which apply here and which determine whether or not the paying company will obtain tax relief on the contributions it makes to trustees.

One common remuneration planning device is to combine payments to an EBT with loans to the employees from the trustees. These loans attract income tax on the employees at a very low rate; much lower than a bonus of the equivalent amount would.

HMRC has challenged a number of EBT structures over the years so great care and specialist advice from an experienced scheme sponsor/provider should be taken before embarking. The use of EBTs should only be contemplated when your business' profits are becoming larger and also if you don't mind taking the inherent risk that some of these deliberate tax planning structures inevitably involve.

For a look at how an EBT might work see Example 9.

Example 9 – Employee Benefit Trust

Tania is a director of a company which provides high level executive training services. She receives a loan of £100,000 from an EBT. The loan will be taxed at the official rate of 4.75%, giving a taxable benefit of only £4,750 on which Tania will probably pay 40% higher rate income tax of £1,900.

This is clearly a very low tax bill on a sum of £100,000 and shows why such schemes are popular. Of course nothing is as straightforward as this and some commentators would say that such strategies are too good to be true. Certainly, you should take very thorough legal and technical tax advice before embarking on this path and weigh up the pros and cons before going ahead. The tax advantages look very attractive but the implications of the use of such a strategy, especially the implications of ending up with a loan from the company rather than an outright bonus, need to be weighed carefully.

Review methods of property ownership

The ownership of company property via a pension scheme as outlined above can prove a very tax effective means of structuring the ownership of valuable business assets. Wherever your business operates from a valuable property asset, you will need to consider very carefully whether or not the ownership of the property is structured in the most tax efficient manner.

Rents can be a useful means of extracting profits from a business, whether incorporated or unincorporated. For the limited company, rents paid to the owner of a property do not carry a PAYE tax or NIC deduction obligation at source. Clearly rents are generally taxable on the recipient property owner/landlord (unless it is a pension fund), so the personal tax position of the recipient should be taken into account carefully.

However, where profits inside your business are considerable, paying yourself rent might well be a useful way of reducing them. If, for instance, the recipient of the rents is a lower rate taxpayer (say another member of your own family) then paying rents out of the company and obtaining a CT deduction could be a sensible structure. If you are the proprietor of an unincorporated business and your personal tax rate is 40%, whereas your spouse who owns the property is a basic rate or even a non-taxpayer, then having the property rented from him or her might also be a sound tax planning strategy.

You should therefore consider at the start-up stage where and how any property assets should ideally be owned. Commonly of course such matters are dictated to you by your lender, who will be seeking some form of security over the business assets (usually the business property) for your borrowings, so it is not always possible to achieve the most tax effective structure here. Additionally it will be important to recognise that some important CGT reliefs are dependent upon the property owner also being involved in the running of the trading business, so again the preferred structure for tax purposes might not always be possible.

Restructure loans and business property borrowings

If you retain ownership of property in use by your business outside the business balance sheet then any borrowings will probably be in your own name as well because they will be secured against the property. This means that you will have to extract funds from the business to enable you to meet the financial obligations, i.e. the repayments and interest on the loan or mortgage secured against the property. A rental could be paid for this purpose but it is important to recognise that where you receive rent from your business to cover the mortgage payments you will need to take the potential personal tax liability into account.

Only loan interest is tax relievable against rents so if the payment you receive in rent is sufficient to cover the entire mortgage repayment element as well, then you will normally end up with a personal income tax liability on the excess of rents above the overheads and running expenses and the loan interest – the capital repayment element is not tax deductible for the landlord.

The location of any borrowings you have for business property assets is an important tax planning consideration for both income and capital taxes. As discussed above, where borrowings on a property that is in your own name have to be paid from your personal funds then you will need to extract funds from the business to enable you to pay the interest and repayments on the loan. Where borrowings are secured on a business property that is in the business balance sheet then these interest elements will automatically be tax deductible against your profits. It is also important to keep an eye on the longer-term tax implications of how your borrowings are structured.

Inheritance Tax (IHT) is charged on the total value of your estate on death, net of the value of any liabilities that you have outstanding. Thus if you own a house worth £1m and have a £600,000 mortgage secured on it then the house is worth £400,000 for IHT purposes. If you have a trading business then under current IHT legislation the value of your interest in the business is eligible for 100% Business Property Relief from IHT. Thus if the net value of your business is £2m this amount would not figure in your IHT computation at all as it should be completely relieved.

If the net value of the business at £2m reflected a factory worth £2.5m and a business loan secured on the factory of £500,000 then the situation is different. For example, if the loan was instead secured on the shareholder's private house, the entire and now increased value of the business would still attract 100% Business Property Relief but the value of the private house would be £500,000 less for IHT, which would result in a potential saving of 40% on the debt – £200,000 in IHT.

Having the loan inside the business achieves nothing for IHT planning purposes. Having the loan secured on a private asset which does not qualify for Business Property Relief reduces the individual's overall taxable estate on death by £500,000, thus achieving a 40% IHT saving (£200,000), so the beneficiaries would potentially receive an extra £200,000 from the deceased's estate.

Restructuring finance that already exists to achieve this saving may not be straightforward but it is well worth considering precisely where your borrowings should be when you take them out, both for the long and the short term.

Be wary of taking loans from your company

If your company lends you money this can have specific tax implications. It is important to be aware of these and also that loans from a private company have to comply with company law, so specific advice will be needed.

When a close company (broadly a small limited company controlled by five or fewer shareholders or by any number of its directors) makes a loan to a participator (broadly defined as a shareholder but there can be other meanings as well) this has tax implications for the company. If that participator is also an employee of the company, for example if you are both a director and a shareholder, then there is a taxable benefit on you as an employee as well.

If a company makes a loan of £100,000 the company has a tax liability of £25,000, which it has to pay to HMRC within nine months of the end of the accounting period during which the loan was made. This tax will become repayable to the company if/when the loan is repaid. If the loan is repaid within the nine month due period then the tax is never payable, but if the loan is repaid after that date then the tax becomes due and is not repayable to the company until nine months after the end of the CT accounting period in which the loan was repaid, which will be one whole year later.

Thus the loan facility might be regarded as a possible means of temporarily extracting funds from a company. Additionally whenever a director or employee receives a loan from their employer they are taxable on the benefit of this financial facility at the beneficial loan rate, which is currently 4.75% for each tax year that the loan remains outstanding. There is a threshold of £5,000, below which there is no income tax charge.

Corporate partnership

The use of a corporate partnership structure is something that may appeal to unincorporated business as profits rise. Under this arrangement, a limited company is added to a partnership as a new partner and then receives a share of profits of the business on which it pays CT rather than income tax. Generally, rates of CT are lower than rates of income tax and so the tax payable on the share of profits allocated to the corporate partner should be considerably lower.

This strategy has a lot of advantages and perhaps offers some businesses a halfway house to incorporation of their business without a complete transfer of an existing business entity to a limited company. If taking this route the business owner should be able to identify a commercial reason for the use of the corporate partner in case HMRC challenges its addition as a partner on the grounds that this is a deliberate tax planning or avoidance device with no other real justification.

Summary

The method by which you choose to extract your profits from the business will have a direct impact on when and how much tax you and the business pay. Different types of business structure involve different extraction techniques and planning options – these must be considered very carefully so that you understand their tax implications and possibilities. The main issues to consider are:

- The structure of the business: sole trader, partnership or company.

- Payment of salary, dividends or a mix of these options (for companies).

- Accumulating profits in the business.

- Pension contributions.

- Structured tax planning strategies.

- A review of borrowings and alternative property ownership structures.

- Addition of a corporate partner to an existing partnership.

Part Three

Withdrawing From The Business And Succession Planning

Introduction

Retirement may not be something you are planning at the moment – it may be a distant dream or a remote prospect – but that doesn't mean you should not give some thought to it even at an early stage in your business career.

Plan early

Very often some of the best long-term retirement tax planning for businesses occurs in the early years when decisions are being taken about business structure. This chapter aims to give you some ideas on these important issues regarding selling your business and retiring.

> " Some of the best long-term retirement tax planning for businesses occurs in the early years when decisions are being taken about business structure. "

Alternatively, if your business is growing and becoming valuable you may be considering how best to realise some of its capital value, either by a sale or by extracting value from it, or you may be thinking of passing the business on to the next generation of your family or to junior managers as part of a planned succession programme.

Whatever your objectives it is important to assess carefully, at an early date, the potential tax implications of when and how disposals of your business and/or your business assets will take place and what tax charges might arise.

Get the best out of the tax regime

The capital taxation regime in the UK is favourable for businesses and some business assets – there are a number of valuable capital taxation reliefs available against qualifying businesses and business assets which it will be important for you to understand. Ensuring that you qualify for these reliefs is essential, or if you do not qualify now then taking steps so that you qualify for these reliefs in the future is very important.

For example, if you qualify for entrepreneurs' relief from CGT this can mean that the rate of CGT that you will pay on selling your business can be as low as 10% on gains up to £5m. If you do not get this right then you could pay 28% (180% more tax).

Review your business structure

Structuring the ownership of your business, whether sole trader, partnership or limited company, is thus crucial to establishing entitlement to this valuable relief. For example, if you alone own the business and the gain is £6m you might be able to save £180,000 by sharing the ownership and running the business jointly with your spouse. The gain assessable on one single individual (ignoring the annual CGT exemption) would produce a liability of £5m at 10% and £1m at 28% = a total bill of £780,000. If the gain was split between two fully qualifying spouses then the whole £6m would be taxable at 10%, giving a liability of £600,000, hence the saving of £180,000.

Similarly, if you qualify for Business Property Relief from IHT then your business assets or shares in your company should receive 100% IHT relief against a lifetime gift to relatives or on your death. However, if your business does not meet some strict criteria for this relief (sometimes it is easy to fall into traps which mean you fail these tests), then you will not get this relief and on a gift to your children you would have to wait seven years for the value of any business gift to pass out of your estate for IHT purposes. Even worse, if you failed to qualify for this relief on your death then a bequest to your children at that time could suffer IHT at 40% instead of being completely exempt. Getting this wrong might mean that your heirs could have to sell some or all of the business in order to pay the IHT.

Clearly, then, it is important to approach the sale or passing on of your business with considerable care so as to ensure that you get the best out of the tax regime. This chapter aims to point you in the right direction with this objective in mind.

9. Sale of the Business

Consider the tax implications of a sale

When a business is sold, CGT may be payable on the profit that you make on the disposal, which will be broadly what you get for the sale less what you paid for the business in the first place.

You may be able to deduct its market value on 31 March 1982 if you purchased it before then, as there is a special rule that operates for assets owned on that date to seek to remove inflationary gains from the charge to tax.

Capital gains tax is chargeable on assets within the scope of the tax. For a business this is broadly all assets such as land and buildings, investments, goodwill, and plant and machinery (although the latter rarely sells at a profit). You will also have a potential liability to CGT if you run your business through a limited company and you sell the shares in

> **"** Capital gains tax is chargeable on assets within the scope of the tax. For a business this is broadly all assets such as land and buildings, investments, goodwill, and plant and machinery. **"**

the company rather than the company selling its assets. If the company sells the assets, it has to pay CT on the chargeable gains it makes and then you personally may have to pay the same tax again when you seek subsequently to extract the net of tax sales proceeds from the company.

For example, if a business sells a factory for £500,000 that it paid £260,000 for originally, then the gain is £240,000. Any incidental costs of selling and buying the property – for example agents' and solicitors' fees and Stamp Duty Land Tax – can be deducted. Improvement costs incurred whilst the property was owned, for example building a new extension or creating new internal offices, can also be deducted. However, no expenses that have been claimed as repairs or otherwise deducted against the annual business trading profits can be claimed again as deductions in the capital gains computation.

The date of a sale is the date that contracts for the sale are exchanged, not the final completion date. This is important as it triggers the timing of the tax liability on any chargeable gain. Capital gains tax is payable by individuals on the 31 January following the end of the tax year in which the gain arises. Corporation tax on chargeable gains is payable by companies along with their other CT liabilities. For small companies this is normally nine months after the end of the relevant company accounting period for tax purposes.

Structure ownership carefully

The way assets are owned is vitally important when it comes to the sale of your business, especially if you are looking to establish entitlement to some valuable business reliefs. If, for example, your spouse owns the business property jointly with you but he or she has not been a partner working in the business, then only you will qualify for the entrepreneurs' relief against your half share. Following changes announced in the 2010 Emergency Budget this can be worth up to £5m of capital gains so it is a valuable relief and great care must be taken not to put it at risk. If your spouse owns

> **If you are planning a sale in the medium-term future and ownership is spread between yourself and your spouse but only one of you works in the business you might wish to consider restructuring either the ownership of those assets or the membership of the business.**

part of the asset but does not work in the business then their share of any gain will be liable at the full 28% non-business rate of CGT, whereas you will probably get some or all of your gains taxed at the reduced 10% rate.

It is thus important to ensure that the ownership and trading status of business assets are properly matched. If you are planning a sale in the medium-term future and ownership is spread between yourself and your spouse but only one of you works in the business you might wish to consider restructuring either the ownership of those assets or the membership of the business. Entrepreneurs' relief entitlement requires at least one year's qualifying status, either as a member of a trading partnership or as a 5% shareholder and an employee of a trading company, so you need to plan well ahead.

Use the available reliefs

For small sales each qualifying individual has an annual CGT exemption, currently £10,100 of gains, so if two or more of you own the business then the sales proceeds and capital gains will be split between you and the tax liability will be lower.

Consider the impact of other tax charges

Apart from CGT, the sale of a business can also potentially trigger other charges to tax. In particular, if your business has been claiming capital allowances against trading profits on plant and equipment for income tax or corporation tax purposes then the sale of valuable plant and machinery items will potentially trigger balancing adjustments that will claw back some of the allowances you have been given previously.

Broadly, when you sell plant and machinery then the sales proceeds (restricted to the amount that you originally paid for the plant items), are brought back into the tax calculations so that a tax charge can arise when the amount brought in like this exceeds the tax value of these items.

> **❝** When you sell plant and machinery then the sales proceeds are brought back into the tax calculations so that a tax charge can arise when the amount brought in like this exceeds the tax value of these items. **❞**

If this is the case then charges to income tax or CT may arise depending upon how you have been running the business. You will need to plan for this.

Apportion sales proceeds accurately

In a business sale one of the most important aspects will often be agreeing the apportionment of the sales price with the potential buyer. There can be opportunities here to mitigate your overall tax liability by judiciously agreeing the sales price correctly in the sales agreement with the purchaser. For example, sales of chattels (tangible moveable property such as fixtures and fittings) can be exempt from the charge to tax on capital gains where an individual item is sold for less than £6,000. This is not always easy to do and there are anti-avoidance tax rules which can come into play, especially if the purchaser is a person connected to you. It is a good idea to get specific tax advice.

Agreeing an apportionment of the sales price of a business disposal which comprises a number of different assets will normally be a job for a professional valuer, especially if the sale is complex and consists of various elements – for example, property and goodwill. It is also important to recognise that buyers and sellers will often have conflicting tax objectives which may be difficult to reconcile. Vendors may, for example, wish to allocate more to the property than to goodwill. The proprietor of a live-in guest house may be able to argue that a significant proportion of their property is relievable from the CGT charge as it has been their private residence.

> " A corporate buyer might wish to allocate a lot to goodwill as tax relief can often be claimed against company profits for this intangible asset, whereas relief cannot generally be obtained for property purchases. "

On the other hand, a corporate buyer might wish to allocate a lot to goodwill as tax relief can often be claimed against company profits for this intangible asset, whereas relief cannot generally be obtained for property purchases. Similarly, in most sales the buyer will want to allocate as much as possible to plant and machinery as they will be able to secure tax allowances via the capital allowances system, whereas a vendor will want to keep this to a minimum so as to mitigate the balancing charges mentioned above on plant sales. In some cases buyer and seller can submit a written election to HMRC to determine the amount to be allocated to these apportionment aspects, but it is important to recognise that objectives will frequently be opposite here and so this can be an important negotiating point in any such transaction.

Available business reliefs

Entrepreneurs' relief

As mentioned already, for many businesses entrepreneurs' relief is the most important CGT relief currently available.

Entrepreneurs' relief is now available against up to £5m of gains per individual business owner. For gains before 22 June 2010 the limit was £2m and prior to 5 April 2010 it was £1m. The relief is given against gains on the disposal of whole or part of a business, or against qualifying gains on sales of trading company shares and (in some tightly constrained circumstances) against gains on personally owned assets used by your business or company. Entrepreneurs' relief now provides an effective rate of CGT at 10% on your qualifying business capital gains.

> **"** Entrepreneurs' relief is now available against up to £5m of gains per individual business owner. **"**

Make a qualifying disposal

For the owner of an unincorporated business it is crucially important to understand what the structure and format of this valuable relief actually means. The relief will be available if you sell the whole of your business but it probably will not be available if you simply sell off some valuable business assets. For example, if a haulier sells its entire fleet of lorries, the haulage depot and the goodwill of the business this will almost certainly be a qualifying disposal. On the other hand, if the business sells off a valuable strip of land at the edge of the lorry park to a local property developer at a handsome profit, this is a simple sale of a business asset and is probably not a qualifying sale of a part of the business.

In some circumstances the value of a specific business asset might well exceed all the value of the rest of the business. In such a case it might even be beneficial to sell off the entire business simply to secure the relief on the valuable asset itself. This may seem strange, but unfortunately tax law sometimes has these rather odd consequences.

Let's look at an example of this situation.

Example 10 – Obtaining entrepreneurs' relief

Joshua is offered £300,000 for the plot of land next to his business, which is situated in a run-down shop on the end of a row of terraced houses. The business and shop premises themselves are valued at only £60,000. If he sells the entire business and the land, which has been used as car parking for customers, he will probably get entrepreneurs' relief against the entire gain. If he simply sells the car park he will almost certainly have to pay 28% on the gain instead of 10%, and as the base cost of the car parking land is virtually nothing this could represent extra tax of about £48,000.

This is calculated as follows:

Sale of the car park alone (ER not available):

*   £300,000 proceeds, taxable at 28%, means tax due of £84,000.

Sale of the whole business, including car park (ER is available):

*   £360,000 proceeds, taxable at 10%, means tax due of £36,000.

£84,000 - £36,000 = £48,000 less tax is due on the combined sale.

Make sure your shares qualify

Entrepreneurs' relief is also available to the owners of shares in an unquoted trading company provided they meet certain conditions; broadly they must have owned the shares and been involved in the running of the business as an employee for more than a year leading up to the date of the sale, and must have owned at least 5% of the shares. The company must have been a qualifying trading company throughout that period as well.

Review minority shareholdings

Where there are substantial minority shareholders who do not work in the business it will be important to look closely at the ownership of their shares and the potential loss of relief arising. If they own less than the required 5% minimum or they do not work in the business then their shares will be taxable at the higher 28% rate on sale.

There are no specific conditions in the legislation defining what is meant by employment so it is conceivable that part-time employment might qualify here. However, this is fairly new legislation, having only been introduced in 2008, so it is difficult to know yet just how aggressively HMRC might choose to interpret these rules.

Review personally owned property

Entrepreneurs' relief is also available against associated disposals. A disposal of a business asset, for example a factory, owned personally by a qualifying shareholder in a trading company can qualify for the relief if this disposal takes place simultaneously with a sale of the shareholder's shares, or in the following three years. Again, this is provided that the shareholding and employment conditions are met.

Here it is also important to mention that if the property owner has been receiving a full economic rent for the use of the property by the company then to that extent the relief will be restricted. Thus in some cases where rental is currently being paid to you by your company, you might want to take advice about stopping the rental payments as receiving these payments can work to your disadvantage where entrepreneurs' relief is concerned. Of course, this may have significant implications for finances if you personally pay the cost of any borrowings secured on the property and these might also need to be restructured at the same time to protect the relief.

This associated disposal aspect of entrepreneurs' relief can also be used to relieve disposals of personally held business assets occurring within three years after the cessation of a business. Note that this does not relieve sales prior to the cessation of trade so it is important to make sure that any such asset sales take place either simultaneously with the cessation of the business or afterwards, not before. Such disposals can normally be relieved when they occur within this three-year period.

Rollover Relief

Some specific types of assets can qualify for a special deferral relief where the proceeds of their sale are wholly reinvested in new qualifying assets within three years after or one year before the sale. The old and the new assets must be used for the purposes of a trade although it need not be the same trade. Land and buildings, and fixed plant and machinery, qualify for this relief, and so does goodwill owned by an unincorporated business owner. Goodwill owned inside a limited company does not generally qualify for this relief.

Where not all the sales proceeds are reinvested then some relief may be available for partial reinvestment, but where the amount not reinvested from the sale proceeds exceeds the computed capital gains then no relief will be available. Actually, the sale proceeds themselves do not have to be used. They could be put towards paying off existing debts and then new borrowings could be utilised to make the qualifying reinvestment. There is no requirement in the legislation to match the actual sales proceeds against amounts reinvested.

It is important to recognise that Rollover Relief is not a permanent relief – the gain is deferred to the time when you sell the new assets. Even so, it is a valuable deferral relief especially for the business owner looking to sell existing premises and reinvest the proceeds along with other money into new larger premises and thus expand their business. It is also a useful relief in as much as it offers a 100% deferral for 100% reinvestment, whereas entrepreneurs' relief does not offer a complete relief. Rollover Relief is also available against gains after any available entrepreneurs' relief is claimed.

Consider deferral relief for non-business assets

A version of Rollover Relief is also available against non-business chargeable gains. Thus, if you make a capital gain on a non-business asset you can get deferral relief if you reinvest in shares that qualify as special trading company shares (known as Enterprise Investment Scheme (EIS) shares). Here the form of the deferral is different in that the gain on the original disposal is computed and then frozen against the day you eventually dispose of the EIS shares. It is then taxed in that later year. You should also take note that EIS shares tend to be inherently very risky.

> " It is important to recognise that Rollover Relief is not a permanent relief – the gain is deferred to the time when you sell the new assets. "

Timing the sale

Pay attention to the contract date

A capital gain is normally a single point in time transaction for CGT purposes. This will normally mean that the disposal is deemed to take place on the date on which you enter into an unconditional contract for the sale. This will normally be the date contracts are exchanged; note this is not the same as the date of completion. It is therefore fundamentally important to realise that it is the exchange date that will normally trigger the timing of the gain and hence the timing of the tax liability.

For individuals CGT is due and payable on the 31 January after the end of the tax year in which the sale takes place. Thus if exchange were delayed from, say, 31 March 2010 to 7 April 2010 the tax would fall due on 31 January 2012 not 31 January 2011; a delay of a whole year.

Income losses may be available for relief

Similarly, ensuring that a capital gain arises in the correct tax year can sometimes mean that income losses can be offset if the taxpayer cannot use them elsewhere.

Income losses on a trading business which are not available for offset against other income can be used in the current year and the previous year against capital gains. Thus if the gain arises in the wrong year then the trade loss may not be available to offset the gain, so timing is crucial.

Time company gains carefully

For companies capital gains are taxed in a specific accounting period. If a gain takes place just before the end of the accounting period then for a small company the CT is due nine months and one day after the end of that CT accounting period. If the gain takes place one day into the start of the next accounting period then the CT is effectively deferred for another year.

On the other hand, if the sale of the asset by a company marks the cessation of a trading business it will be important to recognise that this may well bring the company's CT accounting period to an end. If this is the case then the rate of CT applicable to the accounting period of the gain may rise considerably because the small company CT thresholds are reduced pro-rata by reference to the length of the accounting period.

Thus for an accounting period that is only one month long the small company threshold for marginal rate CT falls to one-twelfth of the £300,000 annual threshold (£25,000) and so it becomes much more likely that the company would pay a higher marginal rate of CT. As such it might then be better either to change the date of capital gain accelerating disposal to the end of the previous 12-month accounting period in order to reduce the CT rate.

Identify when capital losses will arise

Where there are both capital gains and capital losses these can normally be set against each other if they occur in the same tax year for an individual or the same accounting period for a limited company. Capital losses can also be carried forward indefinitely against capital gains arising in subsequent tax years.

However, capital losses cannot be carried backwards to earlier tax years of company accounting periods under current legislation. It is thus crucially important that if an asset is going to be sold at a capital loss you ensure that the loss arises at the same time as or before any other capital gains to ensure optimal offsetting of the losses against the capital gains.

Choose the type of sale – assets or business

Sales can be of business assets, the whole of a business or in some cases partial sales. They can also be sales of the shares in your company or sales of the assets held inside your company.

Where you run your business as a sole tradership or via a partnership then any disposals will be taxed on you personally under CGT rules. Your business gains, subject to entrepreneurs' relief and net of the annual exemption, will now be taxed at 10% up to £5,000,000 of gains and at 28% thereafter. Clearly then, the more people you can involve in the running and ownership of your business the lower your overall CGT liability is going to be on a sale, subject of course to the commercial and personal financial risks that such spreading of your wealth and business ownership will expose you to, as discussed earlier.

Company sales

If your company sells its assets and its business the proceeds will end up inside the company net of CT on the chargeable gain arising to the company. If you then extract the proceeds from the company which now has only cash in its balance sheet then you will potentially suffer tax again on that extraction.

When a company has sold its business you can either extract the net of tax proceeds as income distributions or you can wind the company up and then the capital distributions will be taxed upon you as capital gains as if you had sold your shares. These capital gains in a winding up will normally also qualify for entrepreneurs' relief on your gains provided you meet the qualifying conditions discussed above up to the time your company ceased to carry on trading.

Where the valuable assets are held inside a limited company, vendors will normally seek to persuade buyers to buy their shares because by using this route they will have one sale and one capital gain against which (all other things being equal) they should qualify for entrepreneurs' relief.

If, however, the company sells its assets – land, buildings, etc. – and pays CT on the chargeable gains inside the company, then the net of CT proceeds paid out to the shareholder during a winding up as capital distributions will carry a further CGT charge (hopefully net of the entrepreneurs' relief on the shareholder). This double tax charge is one of the abiding features of the UK's capital gains and company tax system, which almost always introduces an element of conflict into company business sales. Vendors want to sell shares whereas buyers more often than not would prefer to buy assets.

For a buyer, asset purchases do not bring with them the same potential for problems which may arise from taking over the tax history of an existing company and they almost always bring entitlements to valuable tax reliefs such as capital allowances and amortisation tax allowances on goodwill, and possibly also entitlement to Rollover Relief against other previous gains of the buyer. Share sales can bring a multitude of problems. This is the reason why a share purchase is almost always accompanied by a lot more paperwork, including comprehensive tax warranties and indemnities demanded by the buyer.

Where a business is run through a limited company and a sale is being considered, it should be weighed up how much you are prepared to accept for a share sale and how much you are prepared to accept for an asset sale by the company. In many cases, the net of tax proceeds from an asset sale by the company will be significantly less than a share sale will produce. This may even lead to an agreement to accept lower sale proceeds from the buyer as an inducement to agree to a share sale, because this will leave the seller with more money after tax. There is no substitute in these cases to getting an adviser to carefully do the maths for the alternative results for share sale and an asset sale followed by a winding up.

Paper-for-paper exchanges

On some company share sales you may be offered a variety of choices about how to take your sale proceeds. It is common, for example, to see the buying company offering some form of shares or loan notes in the buying company instead of cash upfront. This can be a useful way of deferring CGT liability over several years, subject, of course, to the appropriate assessment of the advisability of this approach and careful advice being taken about the commercial risks entailed.

Broadly, the capital gains relating to the proportion of the sales price taken in loan notes can normally be deferred pending the realisation of the loan notes. It is important, however, to recognise that this can in some cases reduce or even eliminate the amounts of entrepreneurs' relief to which you are entitled so you might merely be sacrificing reliefs to gain tax deferrals. As stated, take advice before agreeing to a paper-for-paper exchange.

Earnout alternatives

On share sales it is also common to see deferred consideration deals and earnout deals under which a proportion of the sales proceeds is paid over time and related to the future results of the business. This is often seen by buyers as a useful way of tying the vendor of a business to the future good health and performance of their business for a medium-term transition period to ensure customer loyalty.

Summary

There are a range of important issues to be addressed when considering a business sale and seeking to minimise the CGT charges that might arise. These are summarised in the following checklist:

- Consider the relative merits of a sale by your company of its assets or a sale by you of your shares in the company.

- Check whether you will qualify for entrepreneurs' relief – if not, find out how to change things around so that you do. Individuals who qualify for entrepreneurs' relief should own the assets and those who do not qualify should not own assets, if possible.

- Think about who owns the business assets. If owners of assets do not participate in the running of the business think about why this is and consider restructuring the asset ownership or the running of the business.

- Rollover Relief may be available if sales proceeds are reinvested. Remember this must be done within one year before or three years after the sale of the assets.

- Consider balancing adjustments that will arise on sales of plant and machinery.

- When will the tax liability arise and can it be deferred by timing the transaction differently?

- Think about offsetting any capital losses – it might be possible to time losses to arise at the right time or before the gains.

- It might be possible to use deferral reliefs against share gains to defer other non-business gains.

- Consider apportionment issues that might arise on the sale – these should be planned and negotiated. Using a tax election may allow sales proceeds to be apportioned tax effectively.

- Thoroughly review the history of assets during your period of ownership to establish specific periods which might qualify for *business use* reliefs.

- You should ensure all improvement costs on assets have been fully identified as these will probably be deductible for capital gains purposes when the assets are sold.

- Some assets can attract favourable CGT treatment so consider whether you can properly allocate some of the business sales proceeds to exempt assets such as moveable chattels.

- Where you are claiming for *use of home as office* consider whether or not this might put the tax relieved status of your main residence at risk over time.

- If you trade through a company keep the status of your shares under review and consider whether or not any investment assets held in the company balance sheet should be removed well in advance of any share sale. If the business is not considered to be trading (and is instead just regarded as an investment activity by HMRC) the tax situation will be affected as valuable capital taxation reliefs will be lost.

- A company might sometimes be able to use pension contributions to reduce the effective rate of tax in the year a profitable sale of its business takes place.

10. Passing on the Business – Successions

Introduction

As you approach the latter stages of your business career, instead of selling your business on the open market as discussed in the last chapter you may decide to pass some or all of the business on to younger members of your family, or to key employees or managers.

The occasion of passing your business over to the next generation is a time for tax planning and consideration of potential tax liabilities. The main problem created by the legislation here is that your family members are regarded as connected persons, which means that transactions between you and other family members are initially regarded as taking place at market values for tax purposes. This can mean that there are potential capital gains and IHT liabilities, and possibly also some income tax issues, to take into account when considering gifts or sales to your relatives.

> **"** There are potential capital gains and IHT liabilities and possibly also some income tax issues to take into account when considering gifts or sales to your relatives. **"**

Passing your business over to younger members of your family will also cause you to consider issues of control and your ability to continue to influence business matters. You may wish to adopt a strategy which enables you to retain some measure of control and influence over the business whilst passing its ownership on.

Fortunately there are some useful tax reliefs available to you so that passing on part or all of a business can be achieved fairly painlessly, provided you have planned in advance. In particular, who owns assets and how they are owned, and the qualifying status of the shares you have in your company if you run the business in this way, will determine the flexibility you have in this planning process.

This chapter offers you a review of the main tax aspects for consideration at this stage and suggests aspects on which you should seek specialist tax advice.

Gifts and/or disposals

Family members

Whenever you make a gift of all or part of your business to any member of your family this could trigger a CGT liability. If the value of what you are giving away is more than the price you paid for it originally, this represents an increase in its CGT value.

Where your own business is concerned, goodwill may be the largest valuable asset (apart from premises or property) that you have, but the goodwill may have cost you nothing. This means the value of the goodwill you are giving away may be *all capital gain*.

You may have run the business through a limited company and here it is quite likely that the shares you own were issued to you at par value, or perhaps they came over to you from your own parents at a very low value. Alternatively, this may be a business you formerly ran as a sole trader and then in partnership before you incorporated it as a stage in its growth. Either way these increases in value could give you a tax problem. This is the case whether you sell the business to your family members or you give it away to them.

Consider employees as well

You may also wish to consider passing your business on to non-family members. You might, for example, have key individuals in the business who you would wish to participate in its future ownership and this may have been the intention for some time. Again there are tax implications to consider here. Specifically, if an employee is provided with gifts of the value of your business, whether this is in shares or assets, or a partnership share, you will need to consider carefully with them whether or not this gives them an income tax liability.

If an employee in a business receives something for nothing by reason of their employment then the tax system may well impose an income tax charge on them as this can be regarded as a benefit in kind. There could also be PAYE obligations on your business to account for this income tax liability, especially where the gift that you make to the employee is in the form of shares in your company. There will probably be a NI charge on the business as well, on the quantum of this benefit charge. So, clearly, transferring ownership to employees can be a costly exercise in tax terms. There are special share schemes and share option schemes that you may be able to use in this situation and you should consult a share schemes specialist to assist with this sort of strategy.

Assess the current values

You will need to get a very clear idea of valuations of the total business and its component assets, both at the time you are selling them and at the time you acquired them. This includes assets, shares, goodwill premises, etc. You cannot assess the potential tax implications without doing this. You may also need to ascertain the same valuations as at 31 March 1982, if you owned the business at that time. The value in March 1982 can be deducted in your capital gains computation in place of the actual historic cost to you if you acquired the assets before that date.

> Valuing a business is not an easy process. A business may consist of property assets, plant and equipment, debtors and liabilities, and perhaps goodwill value over and above the physical value of the assets in the balance sheet.

Valuing a business is not an easy process whether it is a limited company or an unincorporated enterprise. A business may consist of property assets, plant and equipment, debtors and liabilities, and perhaps goodwill value over and above the physical value of the assets in the balance sheet. You will probably have a good idea yourself of what price you might accept for the business if you were to sell it, but it will be important to have professional valuations prepared at an early stage so that you can get a realistic assessment of the scale of the tax issues involved as well, of course, as obtaining a professionally computed valuation of the worth of your business.

Structuring the succession

Of course it is simple to say that you should plan well ahead for this process of handing your business over but it is harder to do in practice. You will need to consider carefully who is going to become more involved in the business, whether they are up to the job and, as a matter of practicality, precisely how the business will be divided and among whom.

You will, in particular, need to give very deliberate consideration to your own future income needs from the business will be and whether sharing business profits with someone else will enable you to fund your own future financial needs and those of your household.

You will also need to decide whether involving the younger generation should be done in the form of a direct share in the ownership of the business from an early stage in its life or simply by providing family members with a share of profits or a salary to begin with and then passing assets over later on. It can be a good idea to provide just some earnings to begin with to see how things go, and then pass on a share of the property, the goodwill or your shareholding later as you begin to see how the recipient settles in to the responsibility of running and managing the business. Transferring assets and shares is an irrevocable step and so should not be approached lightly.

Consider your future income needs

In deciding that you are going to pass some income over to the next generation a first step is to agree what your own future remuneration and profits share from the business is going to be. This is important whether you are running a partnership or a company.

Have a solid partnership agreement in place

For a partnership, the strategy that will be used if one partner withdraws from the business should be set down in a detailed agreement to provide clarity for all parties and to avoid disputes in the future. In a partnership, a partner's salary is simply a drawing for the business so the question of its tax deductibility does not arise (as it would in a company, as discussed later in the section on service agreements). However, a partner's future salary when they leave the business should still be agreed well in advance with the other partners.

Shareholders' agreement

For a company it is a good idea to put in place a detailed shareholders' agreement. Within this, you should quantify your own income needs for the future and determine what mix of salary and dividends you are going to be taking from the business. This has important tax implications, as discussed earlier. Also it can affect the attitude of the tax authorities to the commerciality of the new arrangements you are putting in place.

Having a detailed agreement signed by all the shareholders demonstrates that your salary package and entitlement to income from the company has been the subject of discussion and agreement between all the parties and is not just something that you have imposed on the company unilaterally. Of course, you can only receive dividends if you have shares. You will need to look at the forecast profitability of the company after tax so that you can see if the level of dividends you can expect from a revised shareholding will match your income needs.

Service contract

Establish your profits/remuneration entitlement

A service contract will establish your entitlement to a salary in a situation where you are contemplating making gifts of shares in your company. The agreement will give some degree of continuity and also some security in the event that disagreements arise after the new management is put in place and you have scaled down your day-to-day involvement.

It is important that your right to a future salary is codified in a service agreement in advance of any share or property gifts as this helps to avoid gifts with reservation of benefit problems for IHT, which can arise if you retain benefits over assets given away. Such retentions can mean that the gift you have made is rendered ineffective for IHT purposes.

When an individual gives something away this normally leaves their estate for the purposes of IHT. If they reserve some benefit over what they have given away, for example a right to receive income from it, then the value of what they have purported to give away may still be regarded by HMRC as remaining part of their taxable estate for IHT purposes until that reserved benefit is itself given up.

Also bear in mind that after the share gifts take place you will have a lower entitlement to dividends and so your income from that source will reduce. Once you have identified your personal future income needs from the company your service agreement is the mechanism by which this is secured for the future, so it is vital that it covers all your needs.

The wholly and exclusively test

If running the business through a company, you will need to look at the size of the salary package you are going to receive in the future with an eye on the deductibility of the amount for the business for tax purposes. This is important in relation to the work you are going to be doing for a company because salary and remuneration packages paid have to pass the *wholly and exclusively* test discussed earlier in this book. This is something that is being closely looked at these days by HMRC.

If the service agreement sets out your future salary package and benefits, along with the responsibilities and duties you are going to be taking on, this should serve to establish the entitlement of the company to a tax deduction against your benefits and pay. Of course, it is not acceptable to list roles and tasks that you will not actually be performing in the service agreement.

For the controlling shareholder and director of a small company who is active in running a business it is not usually a major difficulty to demonstrate the hard work being done, but as you take a back seat this might not be so straightforward. Establishing your future roles and responsibilities will be relevant in determining the level of salary you are going to be worth.

Perhaps, having withdrawn from the business, you will have policy-making functions or act as an adviser on business issues, or you may remain in a director's role. In addition, you might be able to demonstrate that your worth to the company and hence the justification for your salary in the future is closely linked to your past experience, your ongoing value as a contact with important customers, and your detailed knowledge of the business.

It may well be useful to have a clause in the service contract and also in any shareholders' agreement stating that you will not be directly involved in setting future increases in your own remuneration package and benefits. This gives some clear indication that you are not reserving a benefit over any shares that you give away in the future after the contract has been put in place.

It is also probably a good idea to have this sort of service contract for the senior shareholder and director to be subject to board review at regular intervals, for example once every five years and even possibly to make it terminable at (say) five years notice on a rolling basis, or alternatively by yourself at your own discretion at any earlier time. This will provide you with some degree of security and these conditions should probably be board minuted and approved.

Pension contributions

If the company is to continue to make significant pension contributions to a scheme on your behalf it will be important to establish the entitlement of the company to tax relief on such pension contributions in the service agreement.

New classes of shares

A tactic in use by some companies is to consider creating different classes of shares for issue to different members of the business as the senior shareholder and controlling director approach the retirement or semi-retirement stage. The issue of a new class of shares can facilitate the payment of dividends in a differential manner to reflect their differing levels of involvement with the business.

For example, the creation of a new class of preference shares issued to you personally would create a right to fixed or preference dividends in the future, thus giving you a clear entitlement to dividends from the company as a prior share of its earnings before other dividends could be declared. This would give you the benefit of a fixed level of income and this is sometimes used to provide the senior shareholder with a level of security instead of the use of an employee service contract.

> **"** The creation of a new class of preference shares issued to you personally would create a right to fixed or preference dividends in the future, thus giving you a clear entitlement to dividends from the company as a prior share of its earnings before other dividends could be declared. **"**

There are of course risks, notably that in bad times a company might not be able to meet the financial commitment that such fixed dividend shares impose on its earnings. There will also be important questions to be answered from the company law aspect as regards whether or not these shares are to be redeemable or not and if so in what circumstances, i.e. during your lifetime or as part of your estate on death.

There can also be tax implications here and expert assistance will be needed. In particular, if you shift value out of some shares into shares of a different class this can trigger capital gain tax liabilities – this can usually be avoided but will need to be planned for.

Share ownership after retirement

The retention of shares in a company after you retire does not immediately create any tax issues. The current capital tax regime in the UK provides 100% IHT Business Property Relief for shares in unquoted trading companies. So long as the company continues to carry on a trade (as opposed to an investment activity) the shares should continue to qualify for this generous relief from IHT if they form part of your estate on death.

This can be regarded as a disincentive for business owners to pass on the value of assets to the younger generation. For partners in a trading business, for example, their shares in the business – their business capital account – qualifies as a 100% relievable asset for Business Property Relief purposes so long as the partner remains active and working in the business. If they retire from the partnership then they can no longer claim this relief. In this respect owners of shares in trading companies are in a somewhat more favourable position. If they retire but continue to own their issued shares in the company then they continue to attract the 100% IHT relief whereas a retired partner in a trading partnership does not qualify for this favourable status.

Available reliefs

There are two important CGT reliefs to consider when planning any business succession. The first of these is entrepreneurs' relief, as discussed in the previous chapter. If you are passing all or a part of your business to the next generation then this relief should be available to reduce the chargeable amount of any capital gains arising on the transfer to connected persons.

Secondly, there is holdover relief, under which gifts of qualifying business assets or shares to connected persons can be the subject of a special tax election between donor and donee. This relief can also be available against deemed gains on transactions which are clearly not taking place at arms length. The effect of the relief is to transfer the capital gains liability to the recipient of a gift (if they are agreeable to this approach) and effectively defer it until they subsequently dispose of it.

Entrepreneurs' relief

As already indicated, entrepreneurs' relief is available against the disposal (which could be a gift) of the whole or a part of a business. Thus if you own a sole tradership or a 50% share in a partnership and make a gift of this to your daughter then such a gift would qualify for the entrepreneurs' relief provided you meet the other qualifying conditions I discussed earlier. Alternatively, if you were to simply transfer a half share in the ownership of your retail premises to your daughter this would represent the gift of a business asset and not the gift of a part of the business so the relief would not be available.

Similarly, if you pass some or all of your shareholdings in a trading company over to a son or daughter then again you should get the entrepreneurs' relief. You would not get this relief if you simply made a gift of an asset which you hold personally outside the business balance sheet as again this is an asset disposal which does not qualify. You would have to transfer ownership of some of your shareholding at the same time, or before the gift, to get the entrepreneurs' relief against an asset held in this way.

It is important to ensure that you will qualify for the entrepreneurs' relief if/when you come to make gifts of valuable business assets or shares in your partnership or limited company over to your children or other family members, if this is at all possible. This is a most valuable relief and can reduce the tax liabilities to a very low level. Timing the transactions and ensuring that you meet the qualifying conditions will be critical aspects of this planning. It is, of course, not essential that the recipient of such a gift is a family member. Entitlement to the entrepreneurs' relief is dependent upon the donor satisfying the conditions for the relief, not the identity of the recipient.

> "Entitlement to the entrepreneurs' relief is dependent upon the donor satisfying the conditions for the relief, not the identity of the recipient. "

Holdover relief

Holdover relief is specifically aimed at helping you to make gifts of your business or business assets to your children so as to facilitate passing the value of the business on down the generations. It is targeted at gifts of businesses and business assets when passing on ownership of some or all of the business.

Unlike entrepreneurs' relief, which provides a reduction from 28% to 10% in the rate of CGT to be paid on a qualifying business gain, holdover relief is a deferral relief. It works by passing the taxable gains over along with the subject of the gift.

Example 11 – Holdover relief

Russ has been running his insurance brokerage business for many years and decides to pass a half share over to his daughter Casey. The only really valuable asset in the business balance sheet apart from some office furniture is goodwill, which is valued at £500,000. This goodwill originally cost Russ nothing when he set the business up 15 years ago as he has built the client base up from nothing himself.

The capital gain on a half share is therefore £250,000. If Russ and Casey together sign a holdover election then no capital gains will be charged on Russ at the time of the gift and Casey will take over Russ's nil base cost. Thus if Casey ever sells her half share of the business she will pay CGT on the gain that Russ has transferred over to her, plus tax on any further increase in value after that date. If the holdover election was not made then Russ would pay tax on the gain arising on the half share and Casey's base cost would be £250,000 for future capital gains purposes.

It is essential when holdover relief is being used that both parties understand the consequences of what is happening. In particular the recipient of the gift should be carefully advised about the potential future tax liability which they are in effect taking on from the donor; indeed they should normally take independent advice here.

In addition to the holdover election described above (made using HMRC form IR295), the parties to such a gift can sign an additional election to submit to HMRC under which the need to value the business shares or assets which are the subject of such a gift can be deferred until the eventual disposal by the donee. This is a useful facility which obviates the need to engage in costly, time consuming and normally unnecessary valuation discussions with HMRC at the time of the gift.

The holdover election can normally be made for business shares, business assets in some situations and shares in an unquoted trading company. The election may also be available for some assets held privately outside the balance sheet of a private trading company where the donor is a shareholder who meets certain qualifying conditions. These conditions are broadly that the donor is employed full-time in the business and owns at least 5% of the shares.

It is important to recognise that this form of holdover relief is only available for gifts of business assets as outlined above. It can also be subject to restrictions if the balance sheet includes non-business assets, such as investment assets. If this is the case then these may well have to be removed from the balance sheet (which might be costly in terms of tax), prior to any such gifts being contemplated.

It will also be important to be aware of how the holdover relief can be restricted if you wish to pass on your business to the younger generation but you are not making a complete gift. It is often a good idea to sell a business share to your children along with a partial gift. This means that you get some cash and they gain some understanding and appreciation of the value of what they are being given.

Where cash does actually change hands it is important to recognise that the holdover relief can be restricted if the amount of this consideration exceeds the cost to you of those assets. Thus, for Russ in Example 11, as he paid nothing for the goodwill, any cash changing hands would restrict the available holdover relief pound for pound. If the goodwill had cost him £100,000, then he could sell £100,000 of assets to his daughter with no restriction to the holdover relief whatsoever, but any proceeds above this would affect the relief.

Use holdovers to trusts for non-business assets

Another form of holdover relief available for non-business assets and also for transfers that are immediately chargeable to IHT is to pass assets over to a family trust for a period of time. This slightly different form of the relief can also be used when you want to pass assets over to the younger generation but do not wish to give them immediate access to the value tied up in those assets. This is commonly the case where a business owner is keen to give the younger generation some involvement and participation in the business, but may not be too keen to put assets at risk for a while. When using a family trust in this way, only the transferor needs to sign the holdover election and the trustees then take on the donor's CGT base cost of the assets against future capital gains on any disposals.

Although this transfer into the trust has to be chargeable to IHT in order to qualify for the holdover relief, it is unlikely to give rise to an actual tax charge as commonly the assets going into the trust should qualify for the 100% Business Property Relief so that the *no lifetime IHT* charge would arise at this stage.

Of course, using a trust in this manner has consequences, not least that thereafter any dividend income arising to those shares will be received by the trust and would probably be liable to tax on the trust at 50%, which will be a significantly higher rate than perhaps it would have been if a direct gift had been made. Additionally, under current legislation such trusts normally have exposure to an IHT charge at a maximum of 6% once every ten years, although here again this should not prove a problem so long as the shares or assets transferred into the trust continue to qualify for Business Property Relief at 100%.

A transfer to a family trust can represent a useful means of making gifts of valuable business assets, whilst at the same time the donor can commonly retain a significant degree of influence and control over what happens to those shares or assets whilst they are inside the trust. The holdover relief available against such transfers of business assets means that no CGT should arise on the occasion of such a gift into the trust.

Summary

There are two potential tax charges that may arise when you pass assets over to your successors:

- Capital gains tax – transfers of valuable assets can give rise to CGT charges.

- Inheritance tax – transfers of valuable assets can trigger potential IHT charges.

It will therefore be important to ensure that:

- You retain entitlement to the valuable CGT reliefs: entrepreneurs' relief and holdover relief.

- There are no investment type assets in the balance sheet which might put entitlement to these reliefs at risk.

- You retain entitlement to IHT Business Property Relief and ensure that there are not assets in the balance sheet which might put entitlement to this relief at risk.

- You retain personal qualifying status and the business continues to qualify as a trading business or company for entrepreneurs' relief purposes. Qualifying status means that as an individual you must be a sole trader or partner carrying on the trade actively yourself, or as a shareholder in your own company you must be employed in the business and own at least 5% of its shares.

- You are involved in the business as an active sole trader or partner and the business continues to be a trading business, for holdover relief purposes.

- You remain actively involved in the running of the business and the business continues to be a trading business, for Business Property Relief purposes.

- You should consider the interaction of entrepreneurs' relief and holdover relief. When you make gifts of assets or shares it is fairly straightforward to use holdover relief to defer the capital gains that might arise. Clearly it is undesirable to defer a larger gain than is necessary, so retention of qualifying status for the entrepreneurs' relief is crucial. However, entrepreneurs' relief simply produces an effective rate of tax of 10% on gains after 22 June 2010, so it may now be necessary to holdover a larger gain than is perceived to be desirable. Obtaining the agreement of the transferees to accepting a holdover election will be a first step in making gifts to your relatives and successors.

11. Implications of Retirement for the Business Owner

A change in tax status

When you retire from active participation in your business your tax status changes significantly. As someone actively engaged in running a business your investment in that enterprise, be it a limited company, sole tradership or partnership, normally qualifies for valuable tax status. After you have retired this no longer applies so retirement can mean that you face extra potential tax liabilities and is thus something to be carefully considered – the advantages and disadvantages should be considered in detail.

Retirement will also inevitably mean that those you have chosen to succeed you in the running of the business, if you are not selling it off, will probably feel that you are no longer entitled to the same level or share in the profits so you will need to assess the desirability of this and what the implications are for your future lifestyle and income requirements.

An investor not a partner

When you leave the running of the business to someone else and cease to be either a partner, sole trader or a working director in your own company you lose your tax status as a participator in a trading business. This means that you are now regarded as an investor for the purposes of assessing entitlement to business tax reliefs on any investment you have

> **If you retire from a partnership and leave some of your accrued capital account entitlement outstanding with the business this is no longer regarded as a trading investment, it is instead a loan to the business with which you were formerly a partner.**

retained in the business, such as equity in a capital account or shares in the company. This is very significant indeed.

If you retire from a partnership and leave some of your accrued capital account entitlement outstanding with the business this is no longer regarded as a trading investment, it is instead a loan to the business with which you were formerly a partner. Similarly, if you retire as a working director and retain some shares in your limited company these are now regarded as mere investment assets.

Reliefs may no longer be available

This means that in the future you will no longer qualify for any CGT entrepreneurs' relief in respect of any disposals of the shares or the capital account if you sell these assets or make gifts of them to connected parties. Clearly therefore you need to consider whether or not you should make such disposals simultaneously with your retirement in order to qualify for these valuable reliefs. Without this relief, capital gains would be taxed at 28%, not the normal effective rate of 10% on most small *business disposals*.

Furthermore, after your retirement your investment in the business will no longer normally qualify for the 100% Business Property Relief from IHT and as such your potential exposure to this liability could increase significantly. You could be exposed to 40% tax liabilities on your investment in the business instead of zero.

Inheritance tax implications

In view of the comments above about the potential loss of valuable reliefs when you retire, many proprietors consider delaying this for some time beyond when it first occurs to them. Indeed there can be a strong argument for simply reducing the level of your involvement in the business but staying on as an active partner or director/shareholder in order to retain access to these valuable tax reliefs.

For example, the partner in a business may simply take a bit of a back seat as they get older but still be involved in the running of the business and in deciding what sort of activities are going to be carried on. Reducing the scope of one's involvement need not mean that you have given up being an active partner altogether. An elderly partner can remain a valuable member of the team running the business for many years. Such an individual might gradually pass over ownership of the business assets over a period of years. So long as the facility to do so with the benefit of CGT Holdover relief remains available this can then be achieved without any CGT arising at the time of these gifts. In this way the elderly partner may retain valuable capital tax reliefs for some years beyond the time when they initially consider retirement, or at least partial retirement.

Clearly this cannot be stretched too far and someone who has completely given up all their active involvement in the running of a business will struggle to retain the business status of their capital account or company shares.

The director/shareholder in a limited company might adopt the same approach. There is no full-time working condition in the IHT rules so becoming a part-time director whilst retaining shareholdings should have the same effect for at least an interim period of years. Active involvement as a working director will be necessary but this need not be at the same level as previously.

The extreme version of this strategy would be to never retire but simply to carry on as a working partner or active shareholder/director until death, thus enabling you to pass on the business assets and shares in your estate free of all IHT as part of your estate. Provided you have continued to meet the qualifying conditions for these reliefs then at that stage 100% Business Property Relief should be available and so no IHT would be charged on your business assets and/or shares.

Similarly, assets will pass to your heirs and beneficiaries free of CGT on your death. Indeed one might say that the current regime of 100% IHT relief and market value uplift on death for CGT purposes gives a lot of elderly businesspeople a significant incentive not to retire. The tax reliefs are a huge benefit but in practice a decision to never retire may not fit in with your personal and lifestyle objectives for your later years.

Review your borrowings again

Part of the IHT planning that you should carry out at this stage will be to review any outstanding personal and business borrowings that you may still have and where these are secured. Of course, the commercial costs and realities of restructuring or refinancing any borrowings should always come first, but it is a good idea to look at exactly where your borrowings are secured and whether or not this is the best place for them for the overall tax position.

Having borrowings secured on qualifying business property may not be the best solution because borrowings secured on private assets reduce the value of those assets for IHT Business Property Relief. This means that borrowings secured on business assets which would otherwise qualify for 100% Business Property Relief are effectively being wasted from the IHT perspective. Of course, you will also need to consider how the finance costs of those borrowings are to be met and whether by you or the business. If you decide to restructure then you should consider what the potential income tax consequences of any financial restructuring package might be.

Consider access to other property reliefs

It will also be essential to consider the IHT position of any property that you own personally but which is currently being used in your business or rented to it. Your retirement from active involvement in the running of a business may affect the tax status of such an asset for the purposes of the valuable capital tax reliefs discussed above.

The controlling shareholder (one who has at least 50% of the voting shares) of a company who personally owns the factory or retail premises that the company trades from may in some situations be entitled to IHT Business Property Relief at a rate of 50% against such an asset. This is unlikely to be the case where rentals are being received. Thus, if at the moment you are content to simply run the company from your own premises without charging rent whilst you are still actively engaged in running the company then this secures you at least 50% business IHT relief so long as you are the controlling shareholder. If you reduce your shareholding below 50% your automatic entitlement to this disappears and your personal exposure to IHT liability consequently increases.

You might decide on retiring that your successors can carry on using the property for its business, but that they ought now to start paying you rent. This will turn the property into an investment asset and again entitlement to any valuable IHT and CGT reliefs would be lost.

If you are to continue to work as a director in a reduced capacity and will also pass on some of your shares to younger members of your family (but will retain at least 5% of the shares) then you should also continue to be eligible for entrepreneurs' relief from CGT against disposals of any property held by you outside the company balance sheet if this property is later sold when you dispose of the rest of your shares. However, if in view of your reduced involvement with the business you decide to charge the company rent for the use of your personally owned premises this will also put this entrepreneurs' relief in jeopardy as the relief is restricted when rentals of this sort are paid.

Timing retirement is important

Plan when to take your pension carefully

The date on which you retire may have a direct bearing on your tax position. Pension schemes will normally have a retirement date built into them which to some extent will determine when you can take your pension benefits. However, you may be able to scale down your involvement with the business earlier than this and you may even be able to access some of your pension funds before this date, although this will require careful advice as this might not be a sound investment decision.

As you approach retirement you should ensure that you have optimised the pension contributions and tax relief regime available to you whilst you are still in business. Once you have ceased in business it will be almost impossible to make tax relievable pension contributions, which means these latter years are an important period when you may be able to boost your retirement income very significantly by making tax relievable pension contributions out of business profits. Once retirement has been taken this opportunity will be lost to you so it is important not to make hasty or rash decisions before you have reviewed the pension position overall. This applies whether or not pension provision is via a personal or an occupational scheme set up through your own company.

> **As you approach retirement you should ensure that you have optimised the pension contributions and tax relief regime available to you whilst you are still in business.**

Time property disposals effectively

Timing issues are always important but can sometimes be difficult to reconcile with other objectives. The ownership of valuable property assets and a desire to sell them as you retire from your business can be a significant problem. Disposals of business assets within an unincorporated trading business will normally qualify for entrepreneurs' relief from CGT and thus achieve a 10% rate of capital against tax where the overall gains are below the current lifetime threshold of £5,000,000.

However, this only applies where the gains arise in conjunction with your withdrawal or retirement from the business. One important issue that needs to be borne in mind is that disposals prior to the withdrawal from the business may well be at risk of failing to qualify for this relief if they are regarded as pure asset disposals not business disposals. To qualify for entrepreneurs' relief the disposal should take place simultaneously with or after your withdrawal from the business. In the latter case the asset disposals should take place within the three years from your withdrawal from the business in order to attract the reduced rate of CGT at 10% on gains below the lifetime allowance of £5,000,000. This can be a problem if you receive an attractive offer for valuable property but this comes before you are ready to retire or significantly reduce your involvement in the business.

Will planning and family tax implications

Introduction

An essential precursor and element of any IHT planning exercise is the drafting of a will in a tax effective manner and also one which is flexible enough and comprehensive enough to cover as many eventualities and desired outcomes as possible. Tax planning inevitably plays a part here but there are a variety of other reasons for making a will as you approach retirement. Indeed, it is advisable to make a will as early as possible during your business career especially if you have children or other dependants.

Non-tax reasons for having a will

You should name an executor in your will. This provides reassurance that someone will take charge of the settlement and distribution of your estate and be responsible for dealing with the authorities, including HMRC. Executors have legal rights and responsibilities and can normally gain access to assets quite quickly and may be able to make interim distributions to beneficiaries with minimal delay. An executor should be a responsible individual and someone who can be trusted by the other members of your family, thus providing them with some reassurance that your wishes are being followed closely.

Without a will, administering an estate can prove time-consuming, difficult and cumbersome. It may be less clear what the legal entitlements of the individual beneficiaries are and it may take a long time to ascertain how many potential beneficiaries are entitled to a share in the estate.

If there is no will it can be difficult for a surviving spouse to gain access to funds for general living costs and he or she may have to seek recourse to benefits from the state as an interim measure until matters are sorted out.

A will can be used to appoint guardians for children where they are still minors and to direct that specific property passes to chosen individuals.

Tax reasons for having a will

Dying intestate can produce undesirable tax liabilities. Where your estate exceeds the statutory legacy for a spouse (currently £450,000 for a widow with no children) the balance goes to other surviving relatives if there are any but without the benefit of any inter-spouse IHT exemption. If there are no surviving relatives the Crown may take the residual estate.

Thus, for example, if an individual dies young and intestate with a surviving spouse and parents but no children and an estate of, say, £1m, the IHT would then be charged on £550,000 at 40%. This is clearly better avoided if at all possible.

Furthermore, the above scenario results in significant assets of value passing to the surviving parents who will be much older. Their potentially taxable estates will thus have been increased unnecessarily and will then incur further undesirable IHT liabilities on their deaths.

General will structuring issues

Marriage

Clearly wills should differ significantly between married and non-married persons. Spouses can pass as much of their individual wealth on to each other as they wish completely free of IHT under current legislation.

Spousal wills should also take account of the facility now available for a deceased spouse's lifetime IHT threshold to be utilised by their surviving spouse.

Spouses – ensure optimum use of the nil rate band

A will should ensure that, as far as possible, the lifetime nil rate band is going to be utilised effectively for IHT purposes between spouses.

Joint ownership is the most common form of ownership found in use for the family home. This will mean that the property passes automatically *by survivorship* to the surviving spouse with no IHT liability. This is by far the simplest means of dealing with the matrimonial home and requires no special provisions to be included in the will. More aggressive tax planning using strategies aimed at the family home should probably be considered as something of a last resort. In recent years HMRC has demonstrated clearly that it is very keen indeed to seek to counter such strategies either in the courts or with new legislation.

On the other hand, the family home often represents a couples' largest single asset of value and may well have to be taken into account if their joint estates are large and likely to provide a very significant and undesirable IHT liability for the beneficiaries of the surviving spouse on their subsequent death.

Under current rules, when the first spouse dies leaving everything to the surviving spouse the lifetime threshold will be available in full to the survivor. Thus on the second death there will be two lifetime allowances available, currently a total of £650,000. If, however, a valuable property asset is owned which is expected to increase very significantly in value then a transfer to other beneficiaries on the first death, still using the individual spouse's lifetime allowance, might take such capital increase outside the estate of the surviving spouse with a consequent IHT saving in the future, on the death of the surviving spouse.

Consider a spousal will trust

Following changes to the taxation of trusts in the 2006 Finance Act, lifetime trusts for spouses may now be treated in the same manner for IHT purposes as discretionary trusts. This means that the settled property may come within the relevant property rules and thus suffer ten-year IHT charges depending on the amount of value settled. Broadly a discretionary trust is regarded as a completely separate taxpayer for IHT purposes. Once every ten years the trust assets may be subjected to an IHT charge, potentially at a maximum of 6%. Furthermore, any transfers out of the trust to beneficiaries can also potentially carry a transfer charge to IHT.

Will trusts of spouses are still regarded as eligible for the inter-spouse exemption provided they meet the conditions for qualification as an immediate post-death interest. This will normally be the case so will trusts should play an important part in any IHT strategy.

A life interest trust for the surviving spouse is commonly used where one spouse wishes the survivor to benefit from assets until their subsequent death. In such circumstances the spouse is provided with security of occupation of the property but the assets can subsequently be passed on to intended beneficiaries, commonly children of earlier marriages. On the subsequent death the assets would then form part of the estate of the surviving spouse for IHT purposes and the benefit of the deceased spouse's lifetime threshold should be available provided it had not already been used on first death of the deceased spouse.

A discretionary will trust may provide greater flexibility of the estate. Gifts out of the trust can be made within two years of the death of the testator and should be regarded as if made on death rather than by the trust itself in many cases.

Passing assets into a flexible trust such as a discretionary will trust on first death may also mean that future increases in value are taken out of the potential charge to IHT on the death of the surviving spouse. Care will be needed to ensure that the needs of the surviving spouse are provided for but it should be possible to draft the trust in such a way as to ensure that the survivor may benefit from the trust at the discretion of the trustees. A letter of wishes or memorandum left to the trustees expressing the detailed wishes of the deceased is normally sufficient to provide the necessary reassurance to the surviving spouse in such circumstances.

Spouses – protect your nil rate bands

The introduction of the transferable nil rate band has arguably made will planning for couples more straightforward. The three chief alternative options are as follows:

1. Leave all property to the surviving spouse. There is no IHT to pay and a full additional nil rate band is normally available on the death of the survivor.

2. Leave all property on life interest trust for the survivor. So long as this is an immediate post-death interest settlement, the same IHT consequences as in (1) above should hold. However, the capital is now protected and can then be passed on to chosen beneficiaries, perhaps children of a prior marriage. Options (1) and (2) could perhaps be combined.

3. Leave those assets which are likely to grow in value so that they exceed the nil rate band, for example valuable property assets, to a nil rate band discretionary trust. Leave other assets to the surviving spouse absolutely.

The surviving spouse – pilot trusts

If the survivor has his/her own nil rate band available the deceased spouse's additional allowances currently bring their joint lifetime threshold to £650,000. If the survivor wishes, they could set up long-term trusts. They might perhaps give consideration to the use of pilot trusts set up during their lifetime. This might be regarded by some as a rather aggressive strategy but where your estate is very large it may well be worth considering. It will require access to specialist advice though.

Pilot trusts avoid the related settlements rules so that property added to them subsequently in several trusts should benefit from each trust having a nil rate band available. Such trusts are set up on different dates. If several trusts are established during life then property could be added on death as well. The effect would be that in future the settled property in each trust is regarded separately for IHT purposes and provided the original settlement was within the nil rate band at that date then the likelihood of future ten-year IHT charges and exit charges is minimised if not completely avoided.

Who dies first – all to each other wills

The mirror-image will, under which spouses both leave everything to each other on first death, is the most common form of will for married couples. It has the benefit of simplicity and ensures that the surviving spouse receives all the deceased assets. He or she can then pass these assets on to children or other beneficiaries in their own will as they see fit. For most married couples with children of only one marriage this normally seems an adequate will plan.

Include survivorship clauses

There can be problems arising in the event of a sudden and unexpected death of both spouses, for example in an accident.

Common property law provides that where two or more persons have died simultaneously rendering it uncertain which of them survived the other, their deaths shall for all purposes be presumed to have occurred in order of seniority and accordingly the younger shall be deemed to have survived the elder. On this basis the estate of one spouse is deemed for IHT purposes to be routed through the estate of the younger spouse in the first instance before going to the children direct.

However, IHT law assumes that where it cannot be known which of two persons who have died survived the other they shall be assumed to have died at the same instant. Thus, the normal effect will be for assets to pass direct to children if spouses die together, for example in a car crash.

More commonly, one spouse might perhaps survive the other after such an accident even if for a short time. Quick succession relief might provide some mitigation of undesirable IHT liabilities in these circumstances. This relief grants 100% relief on the second death in respect of assets received within the previous 12 months. However, the amount of the relief is 100% of the tax charged on the first death, which is not much help as an inter-spouse transfer such as this would attract no tax charge so the relief is nil.

The insertion of a survivorship clause in a will may assist here in some cases.

These clauses normally provide that the estate of the first spouse to die only passes direct to the surviving spouse if he or she survives the deceased by a specific period, normally set at 30 days. If this survivorship condition is satisfied then the law provides that the will clauses passing assets to other beneficiaries, perhaps a will trust as discussed above or other named beneficiaries, are deemed to take effect.

A further rule provides that "where under the terms of a will property is held for any person on condition that he survives another for a period of no more than six months" then in effect IHT liability is held in abeyance and the effects are:

- If the beneficiary (normally the spouse) does survive for the specified period he or she is deemed to have gained their inheritance absolutely as at the death of the spouse.

- If he or she does not survive then the subsequent or reserve beneficiaries (if there are any named in the will) are deemed to have inherited as at the date of the second death.

These provisions should normally produce the result that the assets of the first to die would then only be regarded as passing to the surviving spouse completely if he or she survives their spouse by the specified period, i.e. only if he or she lives long enough to enjoy those assets.

Otherwise any first death provisions included in the will of the predeceasing spouse would come into operation and thus potentially produce a tax saving if amounts in excess of the lifetime threshold are involved.

Summary

The main areas to consider as you approach and prepare for your retirement from business are:

- Be alert to the change in tax status that retirement will entail.

- Try not to lose valuable capital tax reliefs earlier than necessary. Review how your business and private borrowings are structured and consider reorganising them to retain tax reliefs.

- Look closely at the timing of your retirement.

- Consider how passing assets over to your intended beneficiaries will affect your retirement income needs and entitlements.

- Consider carefully your pension entitlements, how this may be optimised and what the timing issues are.

- Have a tax effective will prepared from an early stage and review it regularly.

- Pay special attention to business ownership and structure.

- Pay special attention to the position of your spouse and who owns what as retirement approaches.

Appendices

These appendices provide the essentials of the UK tax regime for small companies and unincorporated businesses. These sections are designed for quick reference and repeat some details from earlier in the book.

Appendix 1: The UK Tax Regime for Small Companies

Outline

UK companies are subject to a separate tax regime from individuals and partnerships and, importantly, are treated as completely separate taxpayers from their shareholders.

The shareholders in a company are taxed as individuals and the company is subject to its own different and separate tax regime from those who own or work within the company. This means that whenever profits or gains are extracted from a company, either as salary, bonuses, benefits in kind or dividends, tax liabilities will arise on those receiving the profits and possibly on the company as well.

All UK companies are liable to corporation tax (CT). If a UK company has any income arising overseas it is still potentially within the scope of UK CT but may also be entitled to claim relief against its UK liabilities for overseas tax under the provisions of a Double Tax Treaty with the overseas country. If there is no such treaty the UK tax authorities may still give *unilateral relief* for the overseas tax on a claim being made in the company's annual CT return.

Tax residence

Liability to UK CT normally arises when a company is tax resident in the UK. A company is treated as resident in the UK if it was incorporated and registered in the UK as a limited company.

If a company is not registered and incorporated in the UK then it can still be treated as tax resident in the UK if it is *centrally managed and controlled in the UK*. This means strategic board decision-making and management by the directors and does not necessarily refer to day-to-day operational management. It is thus possible that a company may trade in the UK but if it does not have a base here and is centrally managed and controlled from overseas then it may not be regarded as tax resident here.

Of course the UK tax authorities recognise that this system might be open to abuse so there are rules which can impose a UK CT charge when an overseas company has a fixed base or permanent establishment in the UK, or when an overseas company trades in the UK through a UK branch or agency which has such a fixed base or permanent establishment.

Definition of a company

A company is defined as *any body corporate* for the purposes of UK CT so this includes limited companies and publicly quoted companies.

Corporation tax is also payable by clubs and associations and similar bodies which, although unincorporated, are regarded as within the scope of CT. The charge can apply to a social club or a golf club if they have income liable to tax.

Mutual concerns

Many small unincorporated associations are only partially taxable as their income arises from transactions among the membership and is regarded as mutual trading, which on case law precedent has been established as non-taxable in the UK. Where a club only has income from its membership its liability to CT is thus likely to be limited to tax on any investment income it earns, e.g. from renting out rooms for functions, and bank or other savings account interest, etc. Clubs and similar bodies will also be liable to CT on chargeable gains arising on any asset disposals, for example if they sell their premises or surplus land, or investments.

Rates of tax for companies

The fiscal year

Rates of CT are set annually in the Finance Act for each fiscal year. The fiscal year for companies begins on 1 April annually. Thus the fiscal year 2011 begins on 1 April 2011.

There are normally three different rates of CT set for companies of different sizes although at times in the past this approach has been varied and changed according to the political climate.

In fiscal year 2011 the CT rate for small companies was set at 20% on all a company's taxable profits and gains arising in the accounting period. A small company is defined as one whose aggregate profits and gains for the 12-month accounting period are less than £300,000. Thus a company with assessable profits and gains of £100,000 will have a CT liability of £20,000.

For more information visit the HRMC website:

www.hmrc.gov.uk/rates/corp.htm

Corporation tax accounting periods

Companies are charged to CT for their corporation tax accounting periods, which is normally the same as the company's financial accounts for a 12-month period. If a company prepares accounts for a period shorter than 12 months then it will be required to submit a CT return for that shorter period.

Where accounts are prepared for a longer period than 12 months the company must submit a return for a 12-month period and then another for the remainder of the period of its financial accounts. A company will therefore normally submit a CT return (form CT600) once a year to declare all of its taxable income and capital gains to HMRC and to facilitate payment of its tax liabilities.

Where a company's CT accounting period straddles 31 March, its CT accounting period must be split into two separate periods and the CT rate applicable to each financial year applied to the apportioned profits pro-rata. Thus if the tax rate changes on 1 April the company will have a hybrid CT rate for its accounting period if it straddles 31 March and will have to apportion its profits in computing its CT liability.

Where the company's accounting period is less than 12 months the small companies threshold of £300,000 is proportionately reduced so a company with profits of £100,000 over a six-month period would pay at 20% as the threshold is halved to £150,000.

The £300,000 threshold has remained the same now for many years. In fiscal years where the threshold changes then the CT accounting period has to be apportioned around 1 April and the applicable thresholds for the two periods are then also applied pro-rata.

Tax payment dates

For a small rate (CT paid at 20%) company CT is normally payable nine months after the end of the company's CT assessable period.

Companies eligible for the marginal relief as described above also pay their CT liability at this due date.

Associated companies

Introduction

Companies under common control are regarded as associated for the purposes of determining the rate of CT applicable to their taxable profits and gains. The effect of this is that the thresholds at which the higher rates of CT become payable are reduced pro-rata according to the number of associated companies that there are.

This is an anti-avoidance measure aimed at preventing business owners fragmenting their activities into multiple companies to take advantage of the lower small companies rate as their profits rise above the marginal rate threshold of £300,000.

Reduced tax thresholds

Thus a company with two other associated companies will start to pay the marginal rate of CT at £100,000 of profits and gains rather than the normal £300,000.

The two associated companies each with profits of £90,000 would both pay tax at the small companies rate of 20% because each profit is below the reduced threshold £100,000. However, two associated companies with profits of £120,000 each would pay CT at the marginal companies' rate with a deduction each for marginal small companies relief computed using the reduced CT thresholds as explained above.

The upper profits threshold of £1,500,000 is similarly reduced pro-rata for the purposes of these comparisons and for the purposes of computing marginal small companies rates.

A company which has two associated companies and whose accounting period to 31 March 2011 is only nine months long would see its £300,000 small rate companies threshold first reduced to £100,000 to reflect the fact that it is one of three associated companies and then again to £75,000 to reflect the shortened accounting period. The upper threshold of £1,500,000 would first be reduced to £500,000 and then again to £375,000.

Common Control

The definition of *control* for the purposes of determining whether companies are associated under these rules is deliberately very broad indeed.

Initially the test looks at control in terms of shareholdings held by individuals. However, it can also take into account other means by which an individual may control one or more companies, namely any rights attached to specific types of shares or by virtue of being a significant loan creditor of a company or also by virtue of entitlement, directly or indirectly, to the majority of a company's assets if it were to be wound up.

Furthermore, in looking to see who is in a position to control one or more companies the tests permit HMRC to take into account the shareholdings or entitlements of other individuals to whom the shareholder has a connection and then attribute those shareholdings to the individual to see if this produces a controlling relationship for two companies. If it does then the companies can be regarded as commonly controlled. The most common connection here will be family, i.e. connections with relatives such as spouses, brothers and sisters, and children or parents.

For these purposes the rules also permit HMRC in some circumstances to take into account the shareholdings held by trustees where there is a relationship between the trustees, the beneficiaries and shareholders in more than one company.

These association tests are drawn very widely so as to seek to prevent businesses from manipulating the availability of the small company tax threshold. However, they can adversely affect the affairs of some businesses which genuinely seek to separate activities into different companies in order to protect themselves from liability claims in commercially risky business areas.

If you are running your businesses through more than one company or considering doing so you will need to take careful advice about the shareholding structure and ownership before proceeding and gain a clear assessment of the extra CT that might arise from simply starting up another company under the same ownership.

The family concession

As a concession, where companies are commonly controlled by family members it is not normally the practice of HMRC to attribute the rights and powers of family members to each other (other than those of spouses and minor children) for the purposes of carrying out these control association tests. Such an attribution will be made, however, where it can be demonstrated that there is substantial commercial interdependence between the companies, i.e. that perhaps one company buys from the other or sells its products to the other.

Substantial for these purposes is interpreted as more than 10% by HMRC. It is also important to recognise that in applying this concession HMRC only looks for dependence of one company on the other, thus the use of the word *interdependence* (implying dependence in both directions) is somewhat misleading.

The irreducible group?

Finally, the concept of common control is also interpreted by HMRC as limited to cases where it can be shown that there is a common irreducible minimum group of shareholders for companies to be regarded as associated.

Thus where two or more shareholders control two companies they might normally be regarded as associated companies. However, if one shareholder can control one of the companies alone and not the other then it cannot be said that the minimum irreducible group of one is the same for both companies. Hence the two companies would not normally be regarded as associated companies for the purposes of CT unless there were other indicators of control such as the controlling individual in the first company having a large loan debt outstanding from the other company, or something similar, which gives him effective control over the fortunes of the second company.

The aggregation of profits and gains

Introduction

For CT purposes all of a company's net earnings from any source are aggregated with the total of its net capital gains and losses arising in the same accounting period to arrive at a global figure of assessable profits and gains for the CT accounting period.

Separate sources have separate rules. A company may carry on a trade which is its only source of income or it may have several different such sources at any one time. They are all potentially liable to CT.

The net assessable amount from each source of income will initially be computed according to the specific tax computational rules applicable to it. Thus rental income, trading profits, investment income, profits on loan relationships (mainly interest income), and any other sources of income arising to the company for an accounting period are all initially kept separate for the purpose of computing the particular amount of net profit arising on each of them.

These separate totals are then brought together in an aggregate figure, to which is added the total of capital gains less capital losses of the year. This aggregate total is the figure to be charged to CT, subject to any deductions for amounts which are specifically allowed against total profits and gains, for example trade losses of the current year or a later year can be used in this manner.

Business profits and commercial accounting principles

Introduction

Tax law provides that business profits are normally to be computed in accordance with generally accepted commercial accounting principles (GAAP). Thus most businesses will need to have their financial profits computed by a qualified accountant. Whilst this is not a legal requirement for the unincorporated business, it is for a limited company.

Limited company accounting profits must be computed in accordance with the *true and fair* view requirements of UK company law and this is also mirrored in the relevant tax provisions. Thus all accounting and applicable financial reporting standards have to be adhered to.

Trading income

- Only revenue as opposed to capital expenses may be charged against trading income in arriving at the profit for each financial accounting period.

- Only expenses incurred wholly and exclusively for the purposes of the trade are charged against profits; this means that expenses having any duality of purposes cannot be charged against trading income either.

Revenue expenses are those that are incurred in everyday running of the business and generally represent the costs of using consumable stores, consuming light and heat and other utilities, purchasing consumables supplies, repairing buildings or plant and machinery, employing staff, and any other general day-to-day running costs.

Capital expenses are those incurred to acquire something new and of enduring benefit to the business such as buildings or equipment, furniture etc. They do not represent the costs of using something up or consuming it but rather are the expense of obtaining something likely to be kept and used in the business permanently.

Thus your company can claim a deduction for hiring and firing staff, renting premises, repairing machinery or heating the buildings it uses, but it cannot claim a direct P&L deduction for buying a new filing cabinet, building a factory extension or installing a new production line. It may in specified cases be able to claim deductions via the separate capital allowances system for certain favoured types of capital expenditures (more detail later).

Dual purpose expenses are not common in a limited company situation and are much more likely to be encountered when a business is run through a sole-tradership or partnership structure. HMRC will examine the purposes of an expense and if it is not incurred wholly and exclusively for the purposes of your business then it is unlikely to attract tax relief.

Where a limited company incurs any personal expense on behalf of the shareholders/directors then this is likely to be treated as a taxable benefit in kind and will be liable to income tax on them as well as being a P&L deduction for the company, so this may not actually be tax effective. The personal income tax liability combined with national insurance liabilities which this will cost the company can in many cases outweigh the CT relief the company will obtain for the expenses.

Other sources

Other sources of non-trading income such as rental income businesses generally follow very similar tax and accounting rules when computing their assessable taxable profits, with some specific changes and alterations as regards certain expenses and receipts.

Adjustments to accounts and accounting standards

There is a plethora of relevant commercial accounting standards which have to be brought to bear in computing accounting profits. Thereafter tax law also prescribes that a range of specific adjustments may have to be made to the commercially computed profits in order to convert that profit into the legally taxable profits.

Thus once an accountant has computed the company's commercial business profits for all its sources of income for the annual financial accounting period he will have to adjust those profits and gains in computing the amount of the taxable profits to be declared to HMRC on the company's tax returns. Thus it is quite common for the taxable profits and gains figure that goes on your company's CT return to be somewhat different from the bottom line shown in your company's financial accounts as the result of these adjustments.

Although no tax relief is given for capital expenses in the computation of profits (thus depreciation is not an allowable deduction for tax purposes and has to be added back in computing taxable company profits), a separate system of deductions does exist for capital allowances on business plant and machinery and a variety of other specifically included capital expenditures incurred by businesses (as discussed in chapter 2).

The importance of GAAP has increased in the last two decades and a number of specific areas of corporate tax practice have been brought more in line with it in order to simplify the tax self-assessment process for companies. In addition there is a long line of tax case judgements in the UK courts that have approved the precedence which accounting standards take for taxation purposes in the UK.

However, it is also important to recognise that where there is a specific tax provision concerning the computation of taxable profits or gains then that will normally override GAAP. Thus whilst it is normal accounting practice to charge commercial depreciation in computing the profits or losses of your company, for example on plant and equipment, there is a specific tax rule which stipulates that in computing taxable profits these charges to P&L must be disallowed.

Similarly there are some tax laws which provide for a deduction in computing taxable profits despite the fact that commercial accounting practice might indicate that the expense should be charged to capital rather than revenue costs, or where such an expense might not meet normal tax rules. Thus a deduction is specifically allowed for taxation purposes for commercial redundancy costs despite the fact that otherwise it might be arguable that such expenses are not the everyday cost of running a business but rather are the costs of closing it down and hence arguably are capital costs not revenue costs.

Rental businesses and income from property

Many companies now make their profits from investing in property to rent, either residential or commercial. Historically the rules for computing profits on rental business differed significantly from those applicable to trading companies but thankfully over the last 20 years they have been brought significantly into line with trading rules and are now very similar.

Most importantly when computing the profits of a rental business the same wholly and exclusively rule is applicable in determining whether or not an expense can be deducted in computing the profits of the rental business. Similarly the commercial rule permitting only revenue as opposed to capital expenses to be deducted in computing business profits is applicable to rental businesses for taxation purposes.

Probably the main difference between rental businesses and commercial trading business for UK CT purposes is the non-availability of capital allowances on plant and equipment. Where the rental business is engaged in the letting of residential property then no capital allowances are available against the costs of purchases of plant and equipment for letting in a residential dwelling. Such allowances may be available for letting in communal areas of housing estates and possibly also with commercial property, e.g. industrial buildings.

Businesses running rental activities may also find that their ability to deduct employment costs for directors and owner-managers is subject to a greater degree of scrutiny from HMRC than trading businesses. Here it is sometimes argued that the amount of managerial time and effort required to run such a business is less than that required to run a trading business.

Furnished lettings

Where a rental business consists of the letting of furnished property the rents received for the use of the furnishings are taxable along with the income from the property itself. If a business also offers other services and facilities to the users of the property, such as laundry, the provision of meals, etc., it is conceivable that in fact the lettings might actually amount to a trade rather than property income and then be taxable on the company as such.

Where a property is let furnished for use as a dwelling no capital allowances are available, as explained above, but two alternative bases for dealing with the costs of providing furnishings and furniture are available. Such expenses can either be dealt with on a renewals basis or alternatively by means of an annual wear and tear allowance.

- Under the renewals basis no tax deduction is claimed for the initial outlay on purchasing such items but the costs of replacing them subsequently is claimed in its entirety against profits as and when it is incurred.

- Under the wear and tear allowance, an annual 10% deduction from gross rents net of council taxes and rates is claimed as an alternative to the renewals basis.

Furnished holiday lettings

There is a special regime currently available to companies which rent out furnished holiday property on a tourist basis. Provided certain specific conditions are met the income is given favoured tax treatment. Such lettings income is in effect treated in exactly the same way as general trading income so that, among other things, capital allowances on plant and equipment may be claimed and any losses arising are treated as normal trade losses.

Broadly the conditions are that the property must be available for letting for 20 weeks in any year and actually let for 10 weeks. Furthermore there must be no long-term lettings to the same person (more than 30 days).

The special tax regime for UK furnished holiday lettings is currently under review, with changes expected in 2011.

Lease and premiums

The UK tax regime provides special rules for dealing with the payment and receipt of premiums under leases and also for the purchase and sale of leases, i.e. when leases are granted or assigned. These can be complex and specialist advice should be sought when such transactions are being contemplated.

The grant of a long lease (broadly one longer than 50 years) is treated in effect as a sale of the underlying property and will normally be regarded as giving rise to a capital gain as if the property had been sold. It is technically a part-disposal of the property however, as the landlord is retaining the freehold reversion. This means that any costs attributable to the acquisition of the property freehold by the person granting the lease have to be apportioned in computing the amount to be deducted in calculating the capital gain. This is done according to a statutory formula which provides that, broadly, the longer the lease being granted the greater the proportion of those costs that can be deducted.

Where a lease of less than 50 years is granted then any premium paid by the lessee is split into two portions with one part being assessed on the recipient as capital gain and one part being assessed as rental income. The shorter the lease being granted, the larger the part which will be assessed as rental income received in advance and the smaller the part which will be assessed as capital gains.

Example A1

A 23-year lease is granted for a premium of £60,000.

The calculation used to deduce how much of the £60,000 is assessed as rental income and how much is assessed as capital gains is:

```
(Length of lease in years - 1)/50 x premium paid
```

Thus, where the premium is £60,000:

```
((23 - 1)/50) x £60,000 = 26,400 assessable as
chargeable gains
```

```
Part assessable as rent received in advance = £33,600
```

Special rules also apply to prevent the avoidance of tax by the payment of reverse premiums or sums equivalent to premiums in particular cases.

Single company loss relief

Trading losses

When a company makes a trading loss, computed according to the tax rules for business profits outlined above, it may do several alternative things with that loss depending upon its particular circumstances:

Carry forward

A loss incurred in a trade may be carried forward to future accounting periods and will be offset there against the profits from that same trade. Any losses carried forward in this way may not be offset against profits from other trades or income sources or chargeable gains in that later accounting period.

Carry sideways

A loss incurred in a trade may be set sideways against other income profits or chargeable gains accruing to the company in the same accounting period. Thus if a company has two or more trading activities being carried on concurrently – perhaps it manufactures and retails furniture – losses incurred on the retail trade can be set sideways against profits on the manufacturing trade in the same accounting period. It is important however to recognise the difference from the treatment accorded to trade losses carried forward. A loss carried forward from one accounting year to the next on the manufacturing trade could not be set against profits from the retailing trade in a later accounting period.

Carried back

A loss incurred in a trade may normally be carried backwards to the immediately preceding accounting period and offset there against total profits and gains of that accounting period. This means that the carry back rules are potentially more generous than the rules for carry forward of losses in that they can be offset in the previous accounting period against profits from different trades or income activities as well as against chargeable gains arising in the same accounting period. There are rules which act to restrict pro-rata the amount of offset in earlier accounting periods if the loss arises in an accounting period shorter than 12 months.

Capital losses

Losses incurred on disposals of capital assets are generally only available for offset against chargeable gains arising to a company in the same or subsequent accounting periods. Capital losses cannot generally be offset against trading profits or other income profits of a company. Thus capital losses can generally only be carried sideways against chargeable gains in the same accounting period or carried forward indefinitely to later accounting periods and offset there against capital gains but not against any other profits.

Anti-avoidance provisions on losses

The UK corporate tax regime provides some specific anti-avoidance rules on loss relief which have to be considered when claims are to be made:

Commerciality

Loss relief is only available for losses incurred when a business is being run on a commercial basis and with a view to profit. If an activity continually makes losses over a number of years it is very likely to cease trading anyway, but otherwise the HMRC might contend that the activity is not being run commercially and seek to deny relief for the losses incurred.

The same trade

Trading losses can normally only be carried forward against the profits of the same trade. Thus it is essential that profits and losses of different activities carried on by the same company can be identified separately and quantified accurately. Losses from one trade can only be carried forward against subsequent accounting periods' profits of that same trade and not against the profits of other trades. Where a company carries on multiple different activities it is important that the earnings and expenses of each separate activity can be properly identified to ensure correct offset of any losses as and when they arise.

Major changes

Where the ownership of a company changes hands and within a period of three years there is a major change in the nature or conduct of the trade then a specific provision can be invoked by HMRC which prevents the carry forward of previously incurred trading losses against profits arising after the change. This is a provision intended to counter attempts at loss buying by companies in circumstances where it would otherwise be difficult to demonstrate that the activities carried on by the company after the change in ownership were substantively different from those carried on prior to the change. HMRC provides a detailed statement of practice on the interpretation of major change in the nature or conduct of a trade on its website:
www.hmrc.gov.uk/manuals/ctmanual/CTM06370.htm

Group companies

Some small business enterprises are run through a group of companies in order to provide more flexible and clearly controlled business management and division of business activities. The UK company tax regime includes some specific tax rules aimed at such groups, mainly to facilitate their treatment as one economic entity for tax purposes. Thus groups can generally surrender some losses among themselves – for example trade or property losses incurred by one group company can be carried across for use against total aggregated profits and gains arising in another group company in the same accounting period.

A group is specifically defined in the CT legislation. In general terms a group exists where one company controls another or where one company controls one or more subsidiaries. There are a number of subsidiary conditions relating to this definition and different levels of control are applicable for certain aspects of the group tax regime.

Normally, 75% control is necessary for trading losses to be passed among companies and more than 50% economic control is needed to transfer assets without attracting a capital gains charge. Control is normally defined in terms of shareholdings but there can be other relevant conditions such as loan relationships among the companies and entitlements to assets on a winding up, etc.

Similarly there are provisions enabling groups to surrender rental business losses, excess charges on income and surplus management expenses between group companies for offset against total profits and gain in the claimant company.

Thus the objective of the group relief regime is to enable companies which are essentially managed together as one economic entity to share among themselves the economic and tax benefits of such losses and excess expenses.

Furthermore, the group relief regime enables companies in groups to pass chargeable assets among themselves on a no-gain, no-loss basis. When a business property is moved from one group company to another then normally no CT charge on chargeable gains will arise and in normal circumstances there would be no Stamp Duty Land Tax charge either.

The above provisions all facilitate the running of groups as one single tax entity but they are subject to some very stringent anti-avoidance provisions which may be invoked by HMRC if it perceives that the group tax regime is being exploited for tax avoidance reasons, especially with regard to capital or dividend transactions. There are a plethora of such provisions and the planning of the tax affairs of groups of companies is a task best undertaken by specialist tax advisers and accountants with significant tax experience in this particular field.

Running a number of business activities together within a group of companies can have clear advantages from the management's point of view. It may well facilitate clearer lines of managerial responsibility and accountability, and enable clearer controls over costs and identification of the profits of different business activities.

Recent changes in tax law may also mean that there can be specific tax advantages as well. In particular the disposal of the shares in a trading subsidiary by the holding company of a trading group can, in certain qualifying circumstances, now be treated as a completely tax free capital gain for the holding company under what is known as the substantial shareholdings exemptions. This exemption is available provided certain key conditions are met, chiefly that the selling company has to be either a trading company in its own right both before and after the transaction, or the holding company of a trading group both before and after the transaction.

Dividend taxation and shareholders

The accumulated profits of a UK company are subjected to CT by reference to the company's CT accounting periods, normally one such period every 12 months. The profits retained in the business after the CT liability has been paid are available for the company to use as working capital in its business. Alternatively those retained profits may be distributed to the shareholders as dividends.

The UK tax system provides that dividends received by individuals are regarded as part of their taxable income. Dividends received by one company from shares it holds in another company are not generally taxed on the recipient company. They are regarded as corporate profits which have already been subjected to CT.

Dividends received by UK companies from overseas shareholdings are also not subject to CT in the UK, subject to certain exceptions. The exceptions are broadly where the dividends originate from a company located in a country which is regarded as an unfriendly tax jurisdiction, which means a country where the UK tax authorities regard there as perhaps being a higher probability that the profits of the originating company may well not themselves have been subjected to tax there.

A UK company may only pay out dividends to its shareholders in accordance with company law. As such it must ensure that it has the reserves available to pay the dividend and that the dividend is properly voted, declared and minuted as such.

When the shareholder receives their dividend it is treated as taxed income in their hands. The dividend is received with a notional tax credit attached, equivalent to one-ninth of the net dividend received. Thus the individual will enter the net dividend plus the tax credit on their personal self-assessment tax return as the measure of their gross income.

A higher rate taxpayer (40%) will then have to pay 32.5% income tax on their grossed up dividend income, subject to an allowance being given for the 10% tax credit.

Thus someone receiving a £9 dividend will be regarded as in receipt of a £10 gross dividend. Their higher rate tax liability (if all the dividend is taxable at the higher rate of income tax) will be £2.25, i.e. 25% of the net dividend.

Under the new 50% top rate of income tax introduced on 5 April 2010 for individuals with income in excess of £150,000 per annum, the net liability of a higher rate income tax payer will become 36.11%, i.e. on a net dividend of £9 received the higher rate shareholder will have further income tax to pay of £3.25 (a not inconsiderable increase in tax liability).

Investment companies

Companies that carry on an investment business rather than a trade are subject to slightly different CT rules in the UK. The most important of these is that a close investment company (defined as one controlled by five or fewer shareholders or any number of directors), will generally be liable to CT on its income and gains at the full 28% rate and not at the small companies rate of 21%. It is thus critically important that the real nature of the company's business is properly understood. Being treated as an investment business can materially affect the rate of tax payable by a company.

There is one important exception to these rules which applies where the investment business carried on by the company is that of property rental. In these circumstances, so long as the property rentals are not to connected parties of the company or its shareholders (i.e. relatives and family members), then the small companies' rate of tax will generally be applicable to the company's rental profits if they are below the small company threshold.

Classification of a company's business as investment activities will have an adverse effect on the status of the company shares for capital taxation purposes.

Someone carrying on a trading business through a limited company can currently dispose of their shareholdings at an effective capital gains tax rate of only 10% on the first £5m of such gains, provided they meet the conditions for the entrepreneurs' relief as discussed earlier. Someone carrying on an investment business through the company will pay CGT on share disposals at the full 28% rate.

Similarly someone carrying a trading business through their limited company will normally be eligible for full 100% Business Property Relief from inheritance tax against the value of these shares on death or lifetime gifts, whereas no such relief is available against the value of shares in an investment company.

Close companies

Companies which are defined as close for the purposes of the UK CT regime are subject to some specific tax anti-avoidance legislation. These rules exist mainly to deal with the possibility that the controlling shareholders and directors might otherwise be able to manipulate the corporate tax regime to their advantage in view of their ability to access the company's funds.

A *close company* is defined in terms of control – it is where a company is run by five or fewer participators (mainly shareholders) or by any number of company directors.

A *participator* is very broadly defined indeed for the purposes of this legislation and can include individuals other than shareholders such as loan creditors and those with entitlements to assets when a company is wound up.

The special tax rules essentially deal with transactions between the company and its participators as follows:

- Any loans or advances made by the close company to its participators will result in a 25% tax charge on the company.

- An Inheritance Tax charge can arise on a company when it makes a transfer of value out of the company's resources to or for the benefit of its participators.

- Benefits provided to participators by the company can in certain circumstances be treated as distribution to the shareholders and hence be taxed as dividends.

- Specific rules can operate to impose an income tax charge on the participators in situations where share benefits are made available to them and these come within the definition of particular tax legislation known as the employment related securities rules. Although these rules are not specifically aimed at the close company it is in this field that they have been most commonly invoked by HMRC.

- Any financial transactions between the company and its participators must be treated as taking place at market value for the purposes of the CT regime as regards capital gains and income tax regulations for both the company and the recipient shareholder.

Appendix 2: The UK Tax Regime for Small Unincorporated Businesses

Introduction

UK income tax is charged on individuals according to their aggregate personal income from all sources. Thus a business owner may also have investment and buy-to-let income as well as their business profits. The total from all these sources is taxed after deduction of permitted reliefs such as pension payments and gift aid donations to charities. The business profits are perhaps just one source of income to be taxable on the individual's annual self-assessment form, albeit often the largest one.

The owners and operators of non-corporate businesses in the UK pay income tax on their profits. Their business profits are aggregated with any other sources of income they have in order to compute the individual's tax liabilities. The taxable amount from each source is calculated according to the specific computational rules for each source stipulated by statute before this aggregation process is carried out. After the aggregated personal assessable income is computed only certain permitted deductions can be made from that gross income figure before income tax is calculated.

Profits belong to the proprietor

The profits of an unincorporated business belong to the owner absolutely and are not treated as accruing to a legally separate entity as is the case for a limited company. Thus the owner of an unincorporated business may withdraw the profits of their business for personal use without any immediate tax consequences. Of course there may not always be funds to withdraw from a business if it is not making profits, so financial and commercial constraints may apply.

The taxable profits of the unincorporated business are thus the amount computed according to the business' P&L account but then subject to any adjustments required for income tax purposes according to the taxing statutes. The profits of the unincorporated business become taxable when they arise and not when the proprietor takes them out of the business.

The self-assessment obligation

Individuals liable to income tax have an obligation to make an annual self-assessment in order to disclose their taxable income to HMRC. Self-employed people running an unincorporated business comprise a large proportion of the self-assessing population. Most taxpayers in the UK do not have to submit an annual self-assessment form as their income is dealt with under PAYE for employment or by deduction of tax at source for pension and investment income.

The proprietor of the unincorporated business has to submit a self-assessment form annually including a summary of their business P&L account and also their balance sheet if they prepare one. Only the largest unincorporated businesses, with turnover in excess of £15million, are legally obliged to actually send in their business' financial accounts to HMRC. All other unincorporated business are required to submit a detailed summary of their accounts on their self-assessment return. The very smallest of unincorporated businesses with turnover below £68,000 p.a. need not submit a full summary of their business accounts annually and may instead submit a simplified financial statement showing turnover, simplified expenses summaries, including capital allowances and net self assessment profits for the tax year.

Calculating business profits

Tax law provides that in the first instance the taxable profits for a business are to be computed in accordance with normal and generally accepted accounting principles (GAAP). Thus most businesses will need to have their financial profits computed by a qualified accountant. This is not a requirement by law for most unincorporated business, whereas it is for a limited company. Certain larger partnerships in the UK and some businesses subject to controls by their regulatory bodies, solicitors for example, are required to have their financial accounts prepared by a qualified accountant, whereas others may choose to do so if they wish.

The profits of an unincorporated business have to be computed in accordance with the *true and fair* view requirements of UK accounting law and this is mirrored in the relevant tax provisions. This means that all the generally accepted financial accounting concepts have to be adhered to.

HMRC will accept the use of simplified accounting methods and procedures by smaller businesses where it can see that year on year the profits are calculated consistently and a reasonable self-assessment result is likely to be obtained. However, for a business of any size it is recommended that an accountant be appointed to prepare the accounts and give advice on the records which should be maintained. It will be of considerable importance to ensure that the fundamental principles of generally accepted commercial accountancy are applied as summarised below.

Principles of generally accepted commercial accounting

The most important principles of commercial accounting for tax purposes are that only expenses properly chargeable against profits are so charged in computing taxable profits. Most importantly this means that:

- Only revenue expenses, as opposed to capital expenses, are charged against trading income in arriving at the profit for each annual accounting period.

- Only expenses incurred wholly and exclusively for the purposes of the trade are charged against profits; this means that expenses having any duality of purpose cannot be charged against trading income either.

Revenue expenses are those that are incurred in everyday running of the business and generally represent the costs of using consumable stores, light, heat and other utilities, purchasing consumables supplies, repairing buildings or plant and machinery, and employing staff and any other general day-to-day business running costs.

Capital expenses are those incurred to acquire something new and of enduring benefit to the business such as buildings or equipment, furniture, etc. They do not represent the costs of using something up or consuming it but rather are the expenses of obtaining something which is likely to be kept in the business permanently or for a very long time to be used for the purposes of the business.

Thus you can claim a deduction for hiring and firing staff, renting premises, repairing machinery or heating buildings, but you may not claim a direct deduction for buying a new filing cabinet, building a shop extension or installing a new machine. You may in specified cases be able to claim deductions via the capital allowances system for certain specially favoured types of capital costs under some specific taxation provisions.

Dual purpose expenses are likely to be encountered when you run your business through a sole tradership or in partnership with someone else. HMRC will examine the purposes of an expense and if it is not incurred wholly and exclusively for the purposes of your business then it is unlikely to attract tax relief. However, HMRC does regularly accept expenses on an apportioned basis where it can be shown that there was a primary business purpose but that perhaps some private incidental or accidental benefit accrued from incurring the expense in the running of your business. The most common expense of this sort would be motoring costs where it is common to see a business journey also involve a small private element.

Tax law also prescribes that a range of specific adjustments have to be made to the commercially computed profits of a business in order to convert those profits into legally taxable profits. Thus once you or your accountant have computed the businesses commercial business profits for your annual financial accounting period you will have to adjust those profits in computing the amount of the taxable profits to be declared to HMRC on your self-assessment tax returns. It is quite common for the taxable profits figure that goes on your tax return to be somewhat different from the bottom line shown in your business' financial accounts as the result of these adjustments.

Although no tax relief is given for capital expenses in the calculation of profits (thus depreciation is not an allowable deduction for tax purposes and has to be added back in when calculating taxable business profits), a separate system of deductions does exist for capital allowances on business plant and machinery and a variety of other specifically included capital expenditures incurred by businesses, as discussed in chapter 2.

The importance of generally accepted commercial accountancy practice has increased in the last two decades and a number of specific areas of income tax practice have been brought in line with it in order to simplify the tax self assessment process for businesses. In addition there is a long line of tax case judgements in the UK courts which have approved the precedence which accounting standards take for taxation purposes in the UK. However, it is important to recognise that where there is a specific tax provision concerning the calculation of taxable profits then that will generally override generally accepted accountancy practice. Thus it is normal accounting practice to charge commercial depreciation in the profits or losses of your business, for example on plant and equipment, but there is a specific rule of tax law which stipulates that in taxable profits these charges to P&L must be disallowed.

Similarly there are some tax laws which provide for a deduction in computing taxable profits despite the fact that commercial accounting practice might indicate that the expense should be charged to capital rather than revenue costs, or where such an expense might not meet normal tax rules. Thus a deduction is specifically allowed for taxation purposes for commercial redundancy costs despite the fact that otherwise it might be arguable that such expenses are not the everyday cost of running a business but rather are the costs of closing it down and hence arguably are capital costs not revenue costs.

Charging income tax on business profits

The proprietor of an unincorporated business, or individuals operating in partnership, must treat their profits for the tax year as one source of income to be included on their self-assessment tax return. When completing your tax form you will need to add a supplementary page for the declaration of your business profits and this will require you to summarise on the return form your business turnover, and its income and expenses for the annual taxable period. These figures will be taken from your annual financial accounts or statements.

The period of your business accounts may not always coincide with the tax year. This depends upon the annual financial year end date you choose when you first start up. There is no law which dictates that you must use the 5 April. Whilst it may be very convenient in many cases it is not always so. For businesses with a seasonal trading pattern there may be another, more convenient date and unincorporated business owners are free to choose whichever annual accounting date they wish.

The general assessment rule for profits

For tax purposes the profits of a business liable to income tax are assessed to income tax on an annual 12-month cycle. The general rule is that a business pays income tax for each tax year on the profits of the 12-month annual accounting period ending in the particular tax year.

Thus a business with an annual year end accounting date of 31 December will pay tax for the income tax year 2010/2011 on its profits of the 12-month annual accounting period ending on 31 December 2010.

Tax payments on profits

Tax for a tax assessment year will be due on 31 January following the end of the tax year, i.e. on 31 January 2012 for 2010/2011. There will also be two payments on account required and these fall due on 31 January and 31 July. Thus a business with a 31 December 2010 year end will pay its first instalment for tax year 2010/2011 on 31 January 2011, the second on 31 July 2011, and the final balancing payment on 31 January 2012.

The annual advance payments on account are set at 50% of the liability of the previous tax year although these can be reduced unilaterally by the taxpayer if assessable income is falling.

Business tax returns

Where a business is run by a single individual they must transfer their business profits onto their self-assessment tax form and include the taxable profits as one source of their gross taxable income.

Where the business is run in partnership, the partnership itself is obliged to submit an annual partnership self-assessment return showing the business' financial statements, P&L account, etc., and also a summary statement showing how those profits are allocated among all of the partners. Each partner then includes on their own self-assessment form a supplementary page declaring their own share of the partnership profits as one source of income for self-assessment purposes.

Rates of tax on business profits

The rate of tax applicable to the profits of the unincorporated business profits for an individual depends upon their gross taxable income. Business profits are taxed as earned income and are aggregated along with all other sources of income to compute the rate of tax applicable.

All individuals resident in the UK (apart from certain individuals using what is known as the remittance basis of assessment for non-domiciled and non-ordinarily resident individuals) are entitled to a single personal tax allowance as a deduction from their taxable income (£6,475 for tax year 2010/2011 although this rises if the individual is over 65) and this is set against their taxable income before applying the relevant rates of tax.

All individuals are permitted a tranche of their assessable income at the 20% basic rate of income tax, (£37,400 for tax year 2010/2011). Thus for 2010/2011 an individual with business profits of £30,000 and no other sources of income would pay income tax on £23,525. All of these profits would be liable to income tax at the basic rate, currently set at 20%.

Once the basic rate tranche plus the personal allowance has been exceeded, i.e. at a profits figure of £43,875 for 2010/2011, any excess profits above this level are currently taxed at 40%.

For tax year 2010/2011 a new higher rate of income tax at 50% was introduced, where an individual's taxable income exceeds £150,000. Further, personal allowances are to be restricted by £1 for every £2 of an individual's taxable income above £100,000, until the personal allowance is completely lost.

Rules for loss relief and available offsets

If an unincorporated business suffers a financial loss the proprietor may be able to utilise that loss in a number of ways to secure tax relief against other income sources and in some circumstances against chargeable gains.

The commerciality tests

Tax law stipulates that only losses arising from genuine commercial business activities are available for tax relief. Thus a trade has to be carried out on a commercial basis and with a view to profit. The implication here is that any business which is not commercially inspired – for instance a hobby or simple pastime – will not be eligible for tax relief.

Certain businesses are also subject to extensions of this general rule. For example, a farming business will not normally be able to claim loss relief where the business suffers losses in successive years for more than six years. This rule was introduced in an effort to seek to prevent the owners of lifestyle or hobby farms obtaining loss relief.

Using loss relief

Loss relief is available in a variety of ways:

Carry forward

A loss in a trade can be carried forward to future tax years and offset there against the profits arising from the same trade. This is the most simple form of loss relief. It is important to note the restriction that a loss on a trade can only be carried forward against the profits of that same trade and not against other sources of profits or income arising in that subsequent tax year. Once a loss is carried forward it is in effect locked in and so can only be used against profits arising from the same trade which gave rise to the loss originally.

Carry sideways

If you make a loss on your trading business in a tax year and you have some other income in that same tax year, for example rents from a buy-to-let flat, you are entitled to carry the loss sideways against your total taxable income in that year thus reducing your gross taxable income in the same tax year that the loss arises.

Carry back

You may also carry a loss back one tax year against your total assessable income for the previous tax year, provided you were then carrying on the same trading activity as currently gave rise to the loss. An extended form of this loss relief carry back was introduced for losses arising in accounting periods ending within the two year period 24 November 2008 to 23 November 2010 as a special measure aimed at helping business through the recession. It enables losses to be carried backwards for up to three tax years up to a maximum amount of £50,000 of loss.

Against capital gains

In limited circumstances you may set off trading losses against capital gains arising on asset disposals in the same year as the year in which the trading loss arises or the previous year.

Carry back against income of earlier years

Where a loss arises in one of the first four income tax assessment years in which you run your business you can claim to carry back that loss against other income arising in any of the preceding three tax years, taking the earlier year first. This can be a very advantageous claim to make as it may provide a refund of income tax from a previous salaried employment which might provide valuable cash flow assistance in the early years of your business.

Carry forward against company income

If you transfer your business to a limited company by incorporation then in some circumstances if you have unused trade losses brought forward you may be permitted to utilise those losses against income, for instance dividends arising to you from the company in the years after incorporation in order to optimise the use of these losses.

Carry forward against NIC liabilities

When you have relieved a loss by carrying it back or sideways against your other income, it can still be carried forward to subsequent years for use against your class 4 NIC profits as charged under income tax rules in the next year. This will not reduce your amount chargeable to income tax in that year but it will reduce the amount on which your business has to pay national insurance on its business profits in that subsequent year.

Terminal loss relief

If a trade loss arises in the 12 months leading up to date on which your business ceases then you are able to carry that trade loss back three years, taking the later year first, and offset the losses against the income there for tax purposes.

Partnership structures

The members of a partnership are generally liable to income tax in the UK on their individual shares of the business' profits. It is important to recognise that if you trade in partnership you are each responsible for your own income tax bills on your own share of the profits.

The partnership itself must submit an annual self-assessment tax return to the HMRC showing how the business profits are to be allocated and this must be agreed formally by all members of the partnership before these returns are submitted. Each partner must then enter their individual share of the profits allocated to them on their own tax return for self-assessment disclosure purposes. This will be the amount on which each partner individually will pay income tax.

It is also important to recognise that each partner is not individually responsible for the tax liabilities of the other partner(s). There is no joint and several liability for each partners' income tax debts as there is for other debts incurred by the business.

It will, however, normally be a very sensible precaution to have the business set funds aside for the partners' income tax liabilities as the years go by so as to ensure that each partner can fund their income tax liabilities as they arise.

Simple partnership

Most partnerships are formed by the drafting of a partnership agreement and the opening of a partnership bank account. This is a simple partnership established under the Partnership Act of 1890. In the absence of an agreement, this is the legislation that governs the running of such a partnership. It is therefore recommended that a proper partnership agreement be drawn up by a legal adviser and signed by the partners so that the financial arrangements for profit sharing and other financial matters are agreed formally between the partners. This can help avoid all sorts of problems if difficulties do arise among partners.

There are two other types of partnership in use in the UK:

1. The *Limited Partnership* provides some protection for partners and limits their exposure to financial losses to the amount of their initial investment. This sort of partnership is also subject to special restrictions for tax purposes as regards the loss relief that partners are entitled to for income tax purposes and broadly limits their loss relief shares to their original financial investment in the business.

2. A *Limited Liability Partnership (LLP)* may also be used and indeed has become much more common in recent years. Such partnerships are used in order to provide the partners with the protection of limited liability and hence lower commercial risk whilst at the same time offering them the commercial flexibility and simplicity of a partnership structure rather than a limited company structure.

Tax on commencement and cessation

Commencement

When a business starts up its profits must be assessed for each tax year that it is in business.

As explained earlier the general rule is that a business must be assessed for the tax year on the profits of the 12-month period of accounting ending in the tax year. Thus a business with a financial year ending on 31 December would have been assessed for tax year 2009/2010 on the 12 months profits ending on 31 December 2009.

However, when a business starts up, special rules operate to tax the profits of the first accounting period.

The profits of the first tax year in which the business trades are always assessed on the profits from the date of start-up to the following 5 April.

The profits of the second tax year are assessed on the normal 12 month accounting date ending in that year if there is a 12-month period to that date. If there is not then the profits of the first 12 months are used for that year.

For the third year the normal 12-month rule is then established.

For worked examples of what this means in practice see chapter 3.

Cessations

When an income tax business ceases to trade, the profits assessable to tax for the final tax year are those computed for the entire period from the end of the basis period for the immediately preceding tax year less any overlap relief brought forward (as explained in chapter 3).

If you run your business as a self-employed sole trader or in partnership with someone else you will have to register with HMRC for the payment of National Insurance Contributions (NIC) on a self-employed basis.

The self-employed individual has to pay two types of NIC to HMRC during each tax year:

Class 2 NICs

A self-employed individual has to make NIC payments at the rate of £2.40 per week and these are normally collected by HMRC via monthly direct debit.

Class 4 NICs

The self-employed individual has to pay additional NICs via the self-assessment tax return system on an annual basis and also via the payment on account system described for income tax above. Class 4 NICs are payable on business profits between thresholds set annually at the rate set in the finance act and at a specific rate above the upper threshold. Thus for tax year 2010/2011, NICs are payable at 8% between profits of £5,715 and £43,875 and at 1% on profits above the upper limit.

Where a self-employed individual's profits are below the lower threshold, currently £5,715, the individual can apply for a certificate of exception and then on this being granted need not pay the weekly class 2 NICs.

Index